TREASURES FOUND IN PASSING

TREASURES
FOUND
IN PASSING

Inspiration for Life's Golden Years

LEONARD MANN

MOREHOUSE PUBLISHING

Morehouse Publishing
P.O. Box 1321
Harrisburg, PA 17015

Morehouse Publishing is a division of The Morehouse Group.

Cover design by Jim Booth

Library of Congress Cataloging-in-Publication Data
Mann, Leonard W.
    Treasures Found in passing : inspiration for life's golden years /
    Leonard Mann.
        p. cm.
    ISBN 0-8192-1880-4
    1. Aged-Psychology-Miscellenea. 2. Aged-Conduct of Life-Miscellanea.
I. Title.

HQ1061.M336 2001
305.26-dc21

00-050100

Printed in the United States of America

01 02 03 04 05 06 07 08 09   10 9 8 7 6 5 4 3 2 1

For Esther,

Who generously gave me fifty-two years of her life
and in the giving added enormously to mine

Contents

Part III

Part IV

Part V

Part VI

Part VII

Part VIII

Introduction

What follows in these pages is designed to be of encouragement and inspiration for people who, like myself, have lived a good many years. Seniors, they often call us.

I should probably let you know that I am indeed a genuine senior. On the day of my birth, Kaiser Wilhelm's German army was marching through Belgium for the invasion of France, the beginning of the First World War, 1914.

Like many of you who may read these pages, I have traveled varied roads, both in dark valleys and on sunlit mountains. Just out of high school, I ventured into the big world at the very depths of the Great Depression and worked for several years at ten and fifteen cents an hour. However, I have later known something of privilege, position, and honor. I have had my share of joys and sorrows, as is no doubt true for many of you.

Everything I include in these pages is wholly original. Some of it comes from my mind and some from my heart; some comes with smiles and some with tears; but all comes with the aim of adding to the joy and meaning and fulfillment of our lives.

Most of what I write will be for the sake of our comfort and well being. Some, however, will have to do with such revelations and discoveries that usually come only to those who have seen much of life and done a great deal of living. A small portion will deal with subjects we older people are inclined to ponder from the vantage of our accumulated years.

This is a volume of short inspirational and insightful pieces, each complete in itself. It will be easy reading, really, but rewarding reading, too, I trust. Bless you, dear friend, as you make your way among these pages and I hope you find the going agreeable and the journey worthwhile.

Part I

If I Never Climb Another Mountain

Rapt, I've stood on mountaintops
  And fingertipped the stars;
I have skimmed ethereal skyways
  In majestic golden cars;
I have known the thrill of summits,
  Spirit high-soaring, free,
Have felt the upward pull of sky,
  Have heard far voices calling me.

And now:

If I never climb another mountain
  Or see those skies again,
Once I did, and to this I hold—
  This I have to glory in.
Nor time or chance can e'er erase
  The touch of angel wings,
The exultant lift of the pinnacle place,
  And the glow that memory brings.

When the Tides Come In

The wizened old man was bearded, barefoot, deeply tanned, and clad only in a pair of soiled cutoffs. As we met at the water's edge on the beach, he bent down and scooped up some object that had washed up on the sand. Holding this with care in his hand, a twinkle in his deep gray eyes, he said to me as I passed, "You never know what the tide will bring in."

1

The old man was right, wasn't he? He was not only right concerning seas and seashores; he was also right concerning these lives of ours. What may the tides bring in? We never know, do we? It is as though we live out our lives on the shore of some great sea, and we never know what the sea will bring to us. The tides rise and fall, they ebb and flow, and there is pleasure and there is pain.

Sometimes the sea is calm, and when we're in a mood for listening, we can hear its soothing whisper. Then, again, there are the storms. With what fury they can come; with what power they can batter our barriers down! Living here as we do and must, we must be poised to greet whatever comes, nor be surprised.

Sometimes treasures wash up on our shores, and we cherish them when they do. Then, too, sometimes ugly things come in, and we wonder why. "Where did that come from," we say, "and why did it come to me?"

You understand, it is not at a static, stagnant pond that we live, but by life's dynamic, surging, ever-changing sea. We never know what the next tide will bring or when the next storm will come. This is what it means to live.

Life is good; and it is all the better for the tides (and, yes, the storms) and for all that they bring. And why? Because we will build a stronger house if it must stand beside a sometimes stormy sea.

THUNDER IN THE DISTANCE

It is a hot, cloudless day in July, and, as a lad of fourteen, I am with my father in the harvest field. There is no sound but that of the grain cradle slashing through wheat stalks and the lesser one as I bind the stalks into sheaves. There is, of course, the barely audible sound of our four booted feet moving inch by inch forward among the stubble.

My father interrupts the rhythmic swing of his cradle, straightens, and with his sleeve wipes the sweat from his face. Then he quietly stands as though listening. "I think I hear thunder in the distance," he says. A little later, he adds, "That is thunder I hear; this means that we'll probably have a storm."

Ready for any excuse to leave our backbreaking task, I suggest that perhaps we should go for refuge to the house. But father says, "We'll never get our work done in the field if we run for shelter every time we hear thunder in the distance." Whereupon, he turns to his cradling again, and I follow with the binding.

There is no storm; we continue working through the day. Low on the horizon there are signs of a storm in the north, but nothing comes near us.

Now, seventy years later, the words of my father are as clear as though spoken yesterday: "We'll never get our work done in the field if we run for shelter every time we hear thunder in the distance."

He was right about that, wasn't he? And what he said is equally as true about life as it is about weather. In matters of health or wealth or other important matters, this or that may seem to threaten us and we may suppose the worst, but only rarely does the worst ever come.

Not all our pains are signs of failing health. Not every dip in the stock market is a precursor of economic disaster. We need always to remember that a rumbling in the distance does not always portend the coming of a storm. We don't have to run for shelter every time it thunders.

The Sound of Bells

Have you seen *The Angelus*, that deeply insightful painting by Jean-François Millet? The scene is a bleak, dreary countryside; the time is day's end. In the foreground stands a peasant couple, a man and woman together dressed in rustic garb, the tools of their labor in their hands. They stand amid the clods and stones of a broken field. Heads bowed, theirs is an attitude of prayer.

In the distance, almost invisible against the horizon can be seen the bell tower of a place of worship. The thoughtful viewer understands that the bells are ringing, pealing forth the signal for evening prayer. Thinking of that distant spire, the artist expressed the hope that all who should ever view the picture would also hear the bells.

In real life, as you and I labor among the clods and stones of our broken fields, it is important that we too hear some distant bells. Most of us need a redemption of our commonplace existence. We need to see beyond our clods and stones and hear the music that comes floating in from afar. Whatever it is that we at this moment must do, life is more than the mundane. It is the distant music that makes the mundane bearable, even joyous.

Whatever the foreground, somewhere on our life's horizon bells are ringing. Above the jangle of telephones, the sound of hammers, the roar of engines, or the beating of hearts, if we listen we can hear. If it's sadness or sickness or trouble or the infirmity of age that is upon us, it is especially then that we ought to turn our faces to the far horizons and listen for the bells. They are there, all right, and they are calling us to see beyond the clods and stones that lie about our feet.

A Thing of Beauty

As the years go by, there is change. Again and again, the familiar must give way to what is strange. Often we begin to wonder: Does anything last? If so, what? Listen now, and let me tell you the following story.

When I stopped to see the old Shanklin place, it had been abandoned for almost forty years. Fields that once had produced prolifically were now overgrown with weeds and brush. The old farmhouse where three generations of Shanklins had lived was still standing, but barely so.

I went in, walking quietly and speaking softly. Here was the "good room" where the family had often gathered. There was the kitchen, and yonder, just outside the kitchen door, was the old well from which the water supply was once taken. On the other side was the long front porch, now all but rotted away. It was where old Mrs. Shanklin sat the day she died.

I saw no life now—none that seemed to belong, that is. Inside, a field mouse scampered across a floor, and outside weeds and briars were growing everywhere. Decayed posts, some leaning at awkward angles and some already down, marked the line of the wooden fence that had neatly bounded the yard. I could see clearly the place where the yard gate had been.

That was about it. That was all that was left—but not quite. For presently my eye fell upon something red, brilliantly red—a large clump, out in the left front corner of the overgrown yard. There, in defiance of the intruding weeds, stood an old-fashioned rambling rose. Some of the branches had died away, but new shoots had grown from the old and were blooming in all the glory of spring.

With admiration and with awe and reverence, I stood in the presence of this living thing. First it struck me as incongruous, then as something akin to the heroic, and then as highly symbolic.

Though abandoned these many years, it hadn't given up. Though there were no longer human eyes to enjoy its beauty, it had kept on trying. There it stood, shaming the weeds around it, unwilling to surrender the place the Shanklins had claimed for it; it was tenaciously holding on. There it stood, though the hands that had planted and tended it had long since been taken away by death. There it stood, a thing of beauty.

I think that on that day the rose bush spoke to me, and this, I think, is what it said: The truly beautiful is slow to die, and though it suffers ill from ugly things, it carries at its fragile heart an enduring quality that will not let it ultimately perish.

OUR BROCKEN TIMES

Among the Harz Mountains of central Germany stands a granite peak known as the Brocken. A variety of legends and superstitions are associated with it. There is the common belief that the place has an ethereal quality about it, that the area is haunted by strange spirits, that it is a mecca where witches gather.

Although the locale is probably not as weird as is sometimes imagined, it is nevertheless the site of a rather remarkable natural phenomenon known as the Brocken Specter. Because of atmospheric conditions, persons and objects often appear much larger than they really are. Huge, dark, and grotesquely misshapen, they can be frightful in appearance, actually terrifying. Even small shapes and movements are sometimes reflected in images of enormous size, these appearing ghostlike in the very atmosphere itself. There, among the mists, a view of the ordinary, thus distorted, has often occasioned great fear or anxiety among people who have lived or traveled there.

Most of us, however, have never been to Brocken, nor will we ever be. Nevertheless, many of us at times come to our Brocken places, and there we see our Brocken specters. In the ongoing ventures of living, we can see shadows in the mists and be terrified. No, nothing is there, but we think something is surely there. Or, if indeed something is there, whatever it is isn't nearly as frightful as it seems to be. Here, small troubles can loom overwhelmingly large. Sometimes troubles that perhaps yesterday would have been easily manageable seem today impossibly monstrous.

We can be certain, when it is so with us, that we have come among the shadows of some new Brocken. Something has gone wrong, and we have let it get us down; everything seems worse than it really is. Here, the very atmosphere around us tends to magnify and distort every potential problem.

When I come to such a time, I am resolved to remember clearly and know beyond question that there are no hostile forces nearly as monstrous as they appear to be. Thus knowing and thus remembering, I will deal with problems as they really are.

The Resting Place

My pioneer ancestors shared the land with the Shawnee, and there was hostility then. For both it was a perilous time—the natives defending their homelands and the immigrants seeking to homestead there.

Later, I was a child among those hills, growing up on the ancestral land, hearing of old times and old ways. There stood the old log house where I was born, as was my father and his father and others before. The house was torn down when I was eight, and here is where this short story begins.

Between two logs, behind the chinking, was found a chain—a chain carved of wood, about five links of it, each link being about an inch and a fraction long.

Who carved the chain we never knew, but it was old, very old. I have thought much about that chain and especially about the person who carved it—someone near the trunk of our family tree, no doubt. The chain served no practical purpose; it was really just a novelty.

Maybe it was my great-great-grandfather who carved it, or perhaps it was his son; it really doesn't matter, I suppose. But surely the carver was somebody normally busy with work in the fields or woods or smithy. Now home at the day's end, his tools put away, his flintlock rifle standing in a corner or resting on its hooks above the door, the carver sits on the porch as the sun goes down, or by the fire if it's winter. He carves, perhaps absentmindedly at first, but soon there is purpose—he will make a chain.

And so he does. With all the burden of labor, with all the uncertainty and insecurity that attend him, with all the danger that is constantly present, he sits quietly and whittles.

Tomorrow he will be with the plodding oxen again, clearing new ground perhaps, his rifle ready for firing and propped by a nearby tree. But tonight he sits quietly and whittles. At the center of him is a strong, deep calm, and into this calm he now retreats. It is restful here.

He has no need to go out to escape the burdens he bears; besides, there is nowhere to go. He must find refuge within himself, and so he does. Here is a fortress of quiet, and into this he retreats for gathering strength. Manually he makes a trinket; spiritually he refuels his soul. Then, soul refueled and plaything completed, he can lay the thing away with a smile and turn to face the struggles of another day.

A man must be strong: the rigors of this wilderness are not for weaklings. The strength must be of muscle *and* of spirit. A man must be big: he must have much substance within him; there must be room for soul. So he will carve of wood a chain; and I will two centuries later hold that chain in my hand—and wonder.

Things of Greatest Worth

The world's great factories produce many things of interest and value. The things of greatest value, however, aren't actually *things* at all, and they aren't made on assembly lines. They are produced only by individual human persons; they reside only within the human spirit and emerge only from the inner dimensions of what we, as persons, are.

Love isn't manufactured by General Motors, General Electric, General Dynamics, or General Foods. But love does have a very specific source; it is produced within the human spirit, and only there is it ever made.

Kindness doesn't grown on trees like apples, that we may go and pluck it from a limb on some convenient harvest day.

Compassion doesn't float around in the ether or come with the light from some distant star.

If such values as love and kindness and compassion are to exist at all in our world, they must originate and have their being within us; there is no other way.

So, who is to produce them? No person in the world is more qualified than you are; you have all it takes. What the world most needs you are as well equipped as anyone to provide.

Some things, perhaps, you cannot do. You may not have the talent for doing them, or the strength, or the skill. But no talent, strength, or skill is required to produce some love, kindness, and compassion in your heart, and to scatter these about like sweet fragrances carried by the winds.

Limitations imposed by age or time might mean that you can no longer wield a hammer, make a dinner, drive a truck, or write a sonnet, but nothing can ever take from you your power to give to the world at least a little of what the world needs most—more compassion, more kindness, more love.

As long as any one of us can create and share in this way, our life is both viable and useful, and no day need ever be spent in vain.

Outwitting the Sparrows

I once observed a battle between a crow and about a dozen sparrows. It was with fascination that I watched this battle in the sky.

The quick, agile, pesky little birds were giving the larger one a most difficult time. Flying around on all sides of him, dashing at him, pecking at him, they were gradually wearing him down. Any evasive action taken by the crow was more than matched by the sparrows. I thought: How long can he survive?

Then, as I watched, the crow seemed suddenly almost to disappear. Instantly, he became only a small black blob, and that blob dropped toward the ground, falling like a stone.

To escape his attackers, the wily bird had abruptly pulled in his wings, folded them tight against his body, and spiraled down in a free fall. Down he came, speed accelerating, tumbling over and over as any nonliving thing might. I wondered if he would ever unfold those wings. But then, not thirty feet above the ground and not fifty feet from where I stood, he did. He made a graceful dive, pulled out of it, leveled off, and disappeared into a nearby clump of trees.

I'm sure that no First World War "dogfight" over France ever displayed a more spectacular maneuver than this one. Looking up, I saw a bewildered cluster of sparrows; there they were flapping about in total confusion. I could almost hear them saying, "What happened? Where'd he go?"

Now, the crow is not exactly my favorite among birds, but I'm sure he's a proud creature, with a good sense of dignity and a preference for winged flight. I'm sure he would prefer not to be chased out of the sky by a bunch of sparrows. I must applaud him, for here was a bird who saw what he had to do, and he did it.

Sometimes we also, somewhat as the crow, must do battle with the sparrows. Now and then, pesky birds descend upon us, and we cannot just ignore them. These have no wings or feathers, but they do have power sometimes to distress us greatly. As that crow was called upon to deal with an unwanted and second-choice circumstance, so are we from time to time.

For instance, we would rather be on the job or the golf course, but instead we must be on a hospital bed. Or we would prefer to sit at the president's desk, but it's our task to work at the loading dock. Often we would choose a smooth path, but ours instead is a rough and rocky one. Being younger, we can wish to have tomorrow today, but there's absolutely no way we can accomplish that. Or, being older, we may wish to have things now as they used to be, and neither can this be done.

But we can learn something from the crow: Here and now, by whatever sparrows set upon, we *can do* what *must be done.*

My Soul Has Been A Harp

My soul has been a harp
  On which a hand unseen
Has laid to with varied strokes,
  Plucking sometime every string.
Skilled harpist he, who knew
  The sounds he sought to make,
Tones he needed, dark and bright,
  Notes of scale from end to end,
Seeking range of tone, no doubt.

He strove, I think, to make a harmony,
  All—blending light and dark in one.
He was forever tuning.
  Why, at last I think I know:
Harmonies are not made with single notes;
  'Tis in the mating of many
That masterworks are born.
  He needed all these, I know.

He lays now the harp aside:
  Made I the music he meant me to?
Came forth the sounds he sought to come?
  Dark thunders that shook my soul,
Bright notes of starlight kin,
  These, all these, and more,
Make they a master's symphony?
  I hope they do.

Health Hazards

We are subjected to a barrage of warnings concerning our health. This
practice or that food will be our undoing, we are told. Every week adds a
few new adversaries to be wary of. These warnings originate from various
sources and, no doubt, from various motivations. If we listened seriously
to all of them, we'd probably suffer the sort of paralysis that fear induces;
it would appear perilous to make another turn or take another step.

Of course, many of these caution flags are well placed; there are indeed activities and substances that damage health, and it is appropriate that we be warned about them. But raising red flags has become a veritable addiction with us. Maybe we love doing it; maybe we love having it done. Whatever the reason, many have taken to the soapbox, and not only in regard to health. Many are shouting about this or that which is about to do us in; we are shown visions of environmental, geological, astronomical, and sociological ogres that stand over us like the Grim Reaper with scythe in hand.

We are called upon to view an endless parade of nemeses. In that parade there are, no doubt, some really dangerous fellows as well as a whole passel of bogeymen. It is often difficult to discern between the serious and the frivolous.

So it appears that in general we have this thing about hazards. We worry a great deal about them, as though striving to make life hazard-free. But can we? Hazards abound of one variety or another; they are everywhere about us.

As for health hazards, let's face it: living can be hazardous to your health! In fact, if you persist in living, keep it up long enough, your health will break down completely! Even if you could escape all other hazards, living itself will eventually do you in! It's a fact; accept it. But don't give up on living simply because of the hazard involved; go right on with it. However awesome the hazard, living is still worth the risk.

WHEN COMES THE FOURTEENTH NIGHT

Nearly two thousand years ago there was a Greek physician named Loukas. Having been aboard ship in a severe Adriatic storm, this good man later wrote an account of those terrible days and nights (see Acts 27:12-44). The story is one of the best pieces of descriptive literature ever written. Only a little imagination is required to see in this story a parable of life.

First is the sailing on a calm, sun-sparkled sea, the south wind blowing softly. The even, level days are like a song.

Then, not long after, comes the storm! How quick the change—the darkening sky, the clouds of roiling black. It's the tempestuous wind called Euroclydon, the most fierce of storms in all its brutal, driving fury, the icy rain, and worst of all, the dark.

Unable to hold course, the ship is driven before the storm, striking sail, but still driven for three days and three nights. There are efforts to lighten the ship, even the very tackling is tossed overboard. For days and nights, scarcely distinguishable the one from the other, the ship is driven up and down in the Adriatic Sea. For many days, neither sun nor stars appear.

Then, when the fourteenth night is come, the ship is in shallow water. There is the sound of mountainous waves crashing against great rocks. The depth is twenty fathoms, then fifteen.

"Throw out the anchors!" a frantic voice shouts. Not from the bow, from which anchors are commonly cast, but from the stern, all four of them. Do not permit the ship to swing about; the shoreline cliffs are too near for this! Hold where you are and wish for the day.

Is this story a parable of life? I think so. We like it when the south wind blows softly, but life isn't always like that. Euroclydon will come, the tempest and the dark. The stars will go out, it will be "the fourteenth night," and you will not be able to tell where you are.

Maybe it's a numbing, blinding bereavement, or a sickness, or a hardship, or a deep personal loss of some kind. It's hazardous to take another step, to do another thing, to make another decision. You cannot bear up before the storm. You are driven; the quicksands and the sharp stone cliffs are near. What should you do now? What should you do when there is nothing you can do?

Well, you cast your anchors. You cast all the anchors you have. You cast your anchors of faith, trust, confidence—every one of them—and you hold where you are. You wish for the day, and you wait for it.

At length the day will come, the dawn will break, the sun will rise, the wind will settle, and the storm will pass. Then you will hoist your anchors, and you will unfurl your sails. You will go on again.

Getting to the Answer Pages

Wherever we are, we always stand at the edge of an unknown. And no matter how far we advance from there, we discover that we still stand precisely at the edge of an unknown.

From two thousand years ago, Esdras gives us this: "The more you search, the more you will marvel." Since then, we have done a lot of searching, and we've done a lot of finding. Just now we have more to marvel about than ever before.

Answers generate questions. No sooner, for example, does science solve a mystery than a score of others stand forth to take its place. Whatever number of days we may have logged and mastered, tomorrow remains an unknown.

Into this picture steps faith. Does it belong? Does it relate? Has it value? What is its role?

Faith makes no pretense of answering all questions. Nor is faith a solution for all mysteries; it does not pretend to be. It does not propose to wipe out all that is puzzling and uncertain.

Faith, rather, is a way of rendering questions and mysteries tolerable, even of making them meaningful and helpful. In a sixth-grade arithmetic book the answers may be found in the back. The book of life, however, does not come with an answer section to which we can turn at will. We must go through this book page by page and wait; we cannot turn to the back to find the answers now.

What, then, does faith do? It lets us know that if we add two and two correctly, the answer pages will confirm our work. It lets us know that if we work through the problems by the rules, we need not worry what the answer pages will say.

Thus, you see, faith arranges things so we don't have to know all the answers now. Faith assures us that if we follow the road, we arrive; all we need know is the way, and we can trust for the end.

The end, of course, is not yet. We are in interval time, interlude; we are somewhere between the front cover and the answer pages. With faith, in spite of all the unknowns, we can go on with confidence.

We will search. The more we search, the more we will marvel, and the marveling will only add to the adventure. The excited anticipation of turning the last page will grow with each new page we turn.

We Color Our Worlds

I gave two children pages of coloring to do—outlines to be crayon-filled as each child should choose. The two scenes were alike—a village street with houses, trees, and flowers growing by picket fences. To each child I gave a large new carton of crayons containing all the colors any child might ever wish. And I said to them, "Pretend that this is the street on which you live."

An hour later the children brought to me the pages showing what they had done. Both had colored in all the spaces, having selected their colors from identical color-banks. Both, I think, were somewhat pleased with what they had done.

But how unalike those pages were! On one, the street's pavement was the color of yellow brick, on the other it was black. One child had put lights in all the house windows; the other had left them dark. The one had chosen the bright colors of spring; the other the browns and umbers of late autumn.

I thought: How like these children we all are! We color our worlds.

In the beginning, we are given broad segments of time and place, and we will put our own unique imprint upon them. There are given to each of us all these blank spaces to fill in, outlines to which we will give some measure of content and character. There is given to each of us this long scroll of days, and we will make something of it. When we have unrolled the scroll to its end, filled in all the spaces, and then rolled it up again, it will bear the colorings we will have given it.

We color our worlds. Some will choose this crayon, and some will choose that. The pictures we make will vary widely. Some will be lighted with bold rays of sun, and others will be dark with cloud or storm. Some of us will put lights in all our windows, and some will leave them dark. Some will make springlike scenes, suggesting life, and others will do otherwise.

At length, having finished with all our colorings, each of us will turn and walk away, leaving our marking for others to see. Person by person, our handiwork will vary widely, the differences will be enormous. Why should these colorings we make and leave vary so much? It's not because some of us were given brighter colors and others were given darker ones. The differences are in ourselves.

You know, of course, that the difference between great art and poor is not in the easel or the canvas or the paints or brushes the artist uses, but in the artist. As I color my world, let this, then, be my aspiration: That I may be such a person that every scene I color may have some beauty in it.

THE INCLINED GOD

Does God hear us when we pray? At any particular time, day or night, there surely must be many calling for God's attention, and there must be times when God might like to say, "Take a number and wait."

Would God ever do this? The ancient Hebrew psalmist thought not. Concerning God and himself, the psalmist wrote, "He has inclined his ear to me." The inclined God! To be inclined is to be sloped or slanted or tilted—in some direction. This ancient writer was very sure about God's inclination. "Toward me," he said. Putting it another way, God is leaned forward listening.

If we may for a moment indulge in a little anthropomorphism, let us visualize the great, good, kind King on his throne, his body bent forward, an elbow on a knee, a hand cupped to an ear, looking eagerly in our direction.

Does God hear us when we speak to God? In this picture, God is actually listening even before we speak. Rather than making us wait, God is waiting for us. One must go though channels to get an audience with the Pope or the president, but God is already there waiting for us to come. What is God's response to our coming? I think God smiles and says, "Welcome! I've been expecting you!"

The Light of the One O'clock Sun

The day was dismal, with a mist of cold rain. Smoke from the city's stacks was not rising but sort of flattening out not far above the ground. Overhead there was only a thick, deep gray.

Waiting at the airport for my cross-country flight, I thought: *What an awful day to fly!* But presently we were on the plane, the engines gave forth their burst of flame, and we began to climb. Our thrust upward was like flying through a starless midnight.

Within minutes, however, there was a sudden burst of light, and our mighty aircraft broke out about the clouds, somewhat as a mammoth prehistoric sea monster might have arisen from the deep. As we then followed our assigned angle of ascent, I somewhat casually glanced down upon those dark clouds I had abhorred from below. *But there were none!*

Everything was bathed in the light of the one o'clock sun. There before us were cloud mountains and valleys; there were ripples and dimples and rolling plains—all sculpted out of cloud, all white or white-on-white, touched here and there by artistic accents of shadow, as though to emphasize the majestic beauty of the cloudscape that stretched out everywhere below.

Yes, these were the very clouds I had seen as so oppressive from their undersides. I was seeing them now from their othersides; I was looking upon them from a different perspective and in a different light.

I thought of our human life and our troubles; I thought of us and our difficulties and problems, and the clouds that sometimes obscure our sky. When they are upon us, we can see them only from where we are; enmeshed in them, we see only their dark undersides. But we need to understand that every cloud has another side, and that side is never like this one.

Now, when heavy clouds are above the airport and town, I imagine what those clouds are like on their upper sides, and I paint mind-pictures of white cloudscapes. No, from here I cannot see them, but I saw them once, and I know they are there. And I have seen the sun!

I have learned this about trouble: When it is upon me, I see only the most immediate side of it; but it has another side, and I know that. So now, however deep the darkness, however dense the cloud above me, I try to see it, whatever it is, in the light of a one-o'clock sun.

THE EVERGREEN

How like some people I have known is an evergreen that stands across the street from our house. Most of its neighbors are deciduous trees that lose their leaves each year with the coming of frost. This evergreen is of modest size, not a towering giant by any means. Nor is it a fledgling either, just sort of average in appearance and dimension.

There it stands, firmly rooted to the ground. It cannot flee for refuge from a winter storm nor seek shelter from the blistering summer sun. It must take whatever comes; and so it does, with apparent fortitude and grace.

Great snows can come, and all its green be covered by heavy decks of white. Its major limbs will bend beneath the weight until the bottommost will even touch the ground; but none will ever break. Come the sun and warmer days, the snow will go away. As it goes, those weighted limbs will right themselves, and all their green will show again.

The tree will sometimes lose a lesser branch, the loss but barely seen among all the rest, as though attendant nature has come with pruning hook in hand to amend and shape a little. Older needles will fall, but new will grow.

Then there are winds, the winter storms that rattle windows and often bring great trees crashing down. But this one stands, though pummeled and mauled, bowing and bending, weaving and waving. When the storm is past, there it is, as straight and tall as ever, with perhaps a few scars where twigs were sundered; but these will heal, and passing, you would never see them.

But the thing that impresses me most about the tree is that it is forever green. Other trees change with the seasons, and this is good, given the kinds of trees they are. It is not in them to be always green. Though they can be lovely in summer, they give up when cold weather comes and wait for warmer days. Not so, however, with the tree that stands across the street from our house.

No matter how heavy the snows, no matter how fierce the winds, no matter how cold the winters, this tree is always green. As I stood near it one recent winter day, I offered up this little prayer: Among people, Lord, and as my seasons change, help me to be an evergreen.

How Deep the Water?

In an earlier time, there was contention in the Ohio River valley between the Europeans who wanted to live there and the Shawnee who already did. On one occasion, a white hunter left his party's encampment and crossed the river, looking for deer or bear. There he was soon among hostile Indians, whose presence made it impossible for him to return to his canoe. Feeling it urgent that he get back to the other side of the river, he plunged in and desperately began to swim for the opposite shore.

In those days, there were many who successfully swam that "dark and bloody river," and there were also those who tried and failed. This fellow, before he reached midstream, was virtually certain he would be among the latter. Although weakening rapidly, he made it past midway, however, and in panic continued to flail away with arms and legs, not so much as a swimmer should, but more like a man fighting some overwhelming foe. Floundering forward, he imagined all that dark water beneath him, sure it would swallow him momentarily.

At last, nearing the shore but utterly exhausted, he was ready to consign himself to the depths. But just then, someone called from the riverbank, "Let down and see how deep it is." This he did, and finding the water to be only waist-deep, he waded out!

While thinking of this true and somewhat amusing story, let us also think a little about life. In our traveling across our span of years, how many times do we think we're in deep water, but really aren't! We often imagine we're in head-deep or more, when actually it's only waist-deep or less.

If we can but cease our fighting and flailing and relax a little, we can discover that solid footing is much closer than we knew. So, let's let down; the water may not be nearly as deep as we think it is.

A Parable of Life

The day began uncertainly, the issue in doubt as to whether it would be cloudy or clear. For a long while during the forenoon a heavy storm cloud hung menacingly in the north, and there were lightning flashes at times.

The storm circled around, however, and by noon the heat had become oppressive, this to be somewhat alleviated by a hailstorm that came a little later. The hail did much damage, shredding the flowers and garden plants. The intense heat returned within an hour, with high humidity and steam rising from the water-sodden ground. Soon, however, the earth dried off a bit, and as the sun descended, so did the heat.

Now, as the day nears its end, all is beautiful here. The sun has just touched the hilltop, its rays outspread, coloring the whole of the western sky. What clouds remain from the day form a gossamer canvas for the sun's rays to paint upon, and this they do.

It is peaceful now and so quiet. The hurried, troubled world seems at rest. A westerly breeze comes with cooling caress; there is a touch of calm. It is as though all the day has been preparing just for this. Soon the stars will come out.

Part II

TALL SHIPS AND SHALLOW HARBORS

Having sailed on many seas, weathered many storms, put in at various ports, and known the exaltation of it all, I think I know what I would like to say to any youth who stands timidly at the shore: Many souls are anchored in harbors that are unworthy of great ships.

How thrilling it is to see a strong ship cutting a straight path through stormy seas! She carries a treasured cargo of persons and things. Undaunted by wind and wave, she holds steadfastly to her course. From her bridge she is guided by skilled hands, and deep inside her hull giant gyroscopes hold her steady. Yonder somewhere, eager eyes are looking seaward, awaiting her arrival; and at last she will round majestically into port. This is what great ships are for; this is what they are made to do.

Another ship may only lie at anchor. Barnacles grow beneath her water-line, and rust eats her hull away. Bilge water lies stagnant in her hold, and vermin scamper unhindered about her decks. Her flags lie folded, gathering mildew and mold since last they flew. She inspires nobody; she lies only as a pathetic memento of what was or might have been or ought yet to be.

So it is with souls—persons of humankind. There are those who dare the storms and chart brave courses on uncharted seas, and then there are those who don't.

Souls are made of seafaring stuff, but too often we anchor them in safe harbors—engines idle, sails furled, never venturing, never daring. Here, in anchored repose, the barnacles grow; while yonder, beyond the breakers, the great wide seas are calling.

A Fear of Knowing

As a child, I was for a while the proud possessor of a small brass ring. Sometimes I wore it on my finger, sometimes I carried it in my pocket, and there was at least one occasion when I had it in my mouth. I well recall the taste of the brass, and I remember that immediately afterward the ring was missing. Unable to find it anywhere, I was certain I had swallowed it, and in my child's mind I knew that if I had indeed swallowed the ring, I would surely die from the effect of it.

I was terrified, too terrified to tell anybody. Frantically I searched, reasoning that if I could find the ring outside my body, this would mean it wasn't inside! I looked everywhere among my stuff, carefully searching all my pockets—all but one, that is.

By the time I got to this one final pocket I was too frightened to look. Other than inside my stomach, that pocket was the only place the ring could possibly be. I was sure that if I failed to find it there, I was doomed.

When I climbed into bed that night, that one pocket was still unsearched. I think I slept none at all. Next morning, fear having mounted to the point of panic, I ventured at last to look. Yes, there in that pocket I found the ring! What needless agony I had put myself through—all because I was afraid of knowing.

That childhood experience is a fair example of a thing we adult persons often do to ourselves. We discover a lump or feel a pain somewhere in the body, and we are afraid to go to the doctor, dreading what the doctor will say. So we worry. Fearing to know the truth, we make ourselves miserable with procrastination and apprehension, all of it gravely accentuated by a paralyzing uncertainty.

Sometimes, in our interpersonal relationships, we have the feeling that there is a tension between ourselves and someone else. We would like to know how that person feels and where we really stand, but we are afraid to find out. So we do the worst possible thing: we avoid the person. We go on miserably wondering how things are, probably imagining the worst. All the while, perhaps the other person, a victim of the same disease, is going through an agony equally as great as our own.

I think I have learned this: An uninformed dread of the unknown can be far more devastating and enslaving than a realistic look at the truth, however unpleasant. This is especially so if the truth can be easily found but because of fear or dread is never sought. So, never be afraid to look in the last pocket!

The Ultimate Trust

Looking back across the landscape of my years, I can see somewhat clearly the roads by which I have come. As I survey that scene, however, a question arises: Among all the roads open to me, did I at every intersection choose the right one? Did I always do the right thing? Well, at some points it's hard to know.

The issues of living are not always simple; at many junctures they can be terribly complicated. Choices between the right and the wrong are often blurred by circumstance. Try as we might to read them, the road signs are sometimes dim or perhaps written in a language we just don't understand.

It is possible, I suppose, honestly to believe we are doing right when we aren't. There is normally much we do not know, and, perhaps worse, a great deal we think we know but really don't.

So here am I atop this summit of my life, looking back upon the odyssey by which I have reached this place. Again and again, along the way, I looked down two roads and chose one. At the time, I believed it to be the right one; but now I wonder. I just don't know.

However, I have this confidence: God knows. I suspect that God is the only one who does. As for me, I am not competent to judge all sins, and this includes my own. I can judge some of them, yes, but all of them, no, for I do not know that much or understand everything that well. For this judgment I suspect that only God is qualified. It would surely be presumptuous of me, looking at my life, to select this or that and say: O God, I repent of it, and of it alone, and judge all else to be okay.

If I thus practice a selective repentance, I will likely leave out some items I ought to put in. If I undertake to draw the line that separates between all sin and all else, I risk putting that line in some wrong places. So I must trust God to know where that line belongs; I must leave the issue with God. This trusting, in fact, may be the ultimate trust.

Therefore, trusting God, I will rest my case with God, and this will be my prayer: O God, in this life of mine, please bless all that you can and forgive the rest.

Being Who We Are

A century and a half ago, Theodore Hook was a rather well-known journalist and humorist in England. One day, observing an elegantly dressed, pompous-appearing gentleman making his way importantly along a

London street, Hook approached the man, bowed, and said, "I beg your pardon, sir, are you anyone in particular?" He then quickly disappeared into the crowd, leaving the man to ponder that question.

Justice Oliver Wendell Holmes of the United States Supreme Court was strolling along an ocean beach when a beautiful and chatty little girl fell in and walked alongside him. After the great man and the child had walked and talked together for while, he said to her, "You can tell your mother that you were walking with Oliver Wendell Holmes." With innocent openness and perfect aplomb, the child replied, "And, sir, you can tell yours that you were walking with Miss Mary Suzanna Brown."

Here we have two persons: a man on a London street and a child on an ocean beach. Which of the two do you like better? Can you tell why you chose one over the other?

Well, let's leave that London man to ponder Hook's question, and maybe if he thinks long enough about it, he can at length figure out who he is. Looking at him, we can't tell; he probably doesn't know either.

But that child! Ah, that child! She's simply Miss Mary Suzanna Brown, no question about that. Whether building sand castles or chatting with one of the nation's most important persons, she is simply Miss Mary Suzanna Brown, she herself, and this is all she is and all she asks to be. A human person, in her personhood the equal of any other, she is who she is, so real, so genuine, so natural, and so buoyantly happy about it.

WINGS OF A NEW MORNING

In a hospital to visit a friend whom I knew to be seriously ill, I said to the nurse, "How is it with Dorothy?"

The nurse replied, "It's terminal." In this way she was letting me know that Dorothy was going to die.

I began then to think about this word the nurse had used, the word *terminal*. I considered the question: What is a terminal? When traveling, what does it mean to come to one of these?

Railroad terminals are places to change trains and from there to go on. At bus terminals, one can change vehicles and continue the journey. Great airports are terminals, at which travelers arrive and from which they can take off for elsewhere.

The nurse was saying to me that my friend Dorothy was coming to a terminal. Her use of the word intrigued me. Was she perhaps saying more than she knew?

May it be, indeed, that death is only terminal—nothing more? May it be that the point of death is merely a terminal place? Is it possible, after all, that death is simply a transition point on the journey where we can lay aside the crutches and canes with which we have limped along and take the wings of a new morning?

THE WHETSTONE

I went into a store to buy a whetstone. Because most cutting tools become dull with use, I felt I needed this device for sharpening mine. The store-keeper and I were friends, so we spent a little time in casual conversation. Also present and joining in was a neighbor who lived across the street.

Hearing my mention of a whetstone, this neighbor said, "Let me give you one of those." As it turned out, this fellow had somehow come into possession of an ancient grindstone of rare and perfect grit. This he had cut into pieces of whetstone size, and one of these he gave to me, saying as he did so, "This will last the rest of your life."

That was fifty-one years ago. For more than half a century that stone has served me well. I still have it, but it is now virtually used up. You see, in the long process of sharpening many blades, that stone itself has been worn away. Now it is precariously thin, at the point of breaking apart at any time.

So the whetstone that was to last the rest of my life is now almost gone! It has been worn away by long use. But if not this, then what are whetstones for? And life, what is it for?

If, in fulfilling its purpose, a thing must suffer wear, what is wrong with this? Therefore, having now come to trifocals, false teeth, and arthritis, I observe (with a smile) that my well-worn whetstone is getting terribly thin! After all, the friend who gave it to me never promised that it would last forever.

THE URGE FROM WITHIN

In our garden one day in spring, I noted that a bean sprout had pushed its way through the soil. A couple of small clods, still showing moisture on their undersides, had been rolled over and slightly pushed away. That persistent little sprout, appearing so fragile a thing, had bucked its way up through the hard earth, its pod-head bent down to make a shoulder for pushing. Now that it had broken through the surface, the pod was just beginning to unbend and extend itself to the light.

Carefully, I pushed the clods away and traced that frail stem down through three inches of cool, hard dirt. I saw how it had split in half the brown seed-bean from which it sprang. I saw how it had made its way around a pebble or two, threading itself ever upward, as is the nature of bean sprouts to do. I marveled at the power that made it rise, boring its way though, responding to the upward summons of light.

With a reverent respect for this living thing, I pulverized the clods between my fingers and, with surgical care, packed the soft earth around the slender body in the hope that it might live.

I thought of our human life. There is something of bean-sprout quality in every one of us; we cannot escape it. As there is something in the morning glory that causes it to respond to the caress of the sun, there is something in us. As there is something in the rosebud that urges it to open, there is something in us.

If there is within us, as it seems all too clear there is, that which does not want to respond to an upward call, there is also within us that which will never rest until it can.

His Final and Finest Gift

I once met a widow whose greatest source of comfort was the husband who had just yesterday died. Learning of the death, I felt it my duty on this day to call in the home. Ringing the doorbell, I thought: What a shattering experience for this woman!

But the beautiful, neatly dressed, middle-aged lady who opened the door gave no impression at all of being shattered. As the two of us sat in her living room and talked, I was increasingly amazed by her calm and poised demeanor. I recalled hearing other new widows say concerning their deceased husbands, "He left me well fixed," meaning by this that the husband had provided a kind of survival kit in the form of a substantial economic package—in other words, money.

I allowed myself to suspect that something of this sort might be a factor here. However, as I was soon to learn, I should never have permitted that thought to enter my mind. This woman was genuinely controlled and radiant, projecting a calmness that seemed to come from deep within her. When she told me the secret—and she did tell me—it had nothing at all to do with the family purse; it had a lot to do with something infinitely more important. It had to do with probably the finest gift anyone can ever give to one who is loved.

Here is what this new-made widow said to me: "My husband was a good man in every way, and good to me, always thoughtful of me. He was a very quiet man, a man who never said very much, especially about the deeper things of life. But about a year ago, I noticed that he began to talk more about these things. As I think of it now, he made a special point of speaking often about his religious faith, how much his faith meant to him, how sure he was of God's love and forgiveness, and how grateful. He spoke often of our good life together and of his confidence for life beyond death. I didn't realize until yesterday, when this suddenly happened, that during all this time he was thoughtfully and purposefully doing a fine thing for me. He had known that one day, perhaps soon, I would have to give him up, and he was giving me something to give him up to."

A Point to Ponder

Forrest was a good man and a good friend. His wife died and he was left to wrestle with his loss. To relieve the monotony of long days alone, he invited a much younger friend to move in and share the house with him. During this time he was valiantly struggling up from the valley of shadow, attempting to make reconciliation with the reality of his wife's death.

One morning at breakfast, deeply discouraged and depressed, Forrest spoke of his feelings to his young friend, saying, "I have tried so hard to let my wife go, to accept her going, to adjust myself to getting along without her, and sometimes I feel I've done very well. But you know, this morning if I had the power to call her back, I would."

Without hesitation, the younger man looked across the table into the eyes of the older and said, "But, Forrest, don't you know that if you had the *power* to call her back, you would *also* have the *wisdom* not to do it."

It is now a good many years since my friend told me of this breakfast-table conversation. During this long interval, I have considered and reconsidered the remarkable dimension of the thing that the young man said. What do you make of it?

Of Kites and Life

One sunny day in April, I learned a big lesson from a small boy. I do not believe he intended to teach me anything; in fact, I suspect he scarcely knew I was there. But there I was, leaning against a fence post and rather idly watching as he skillfully manipulated a big red and white kite he was flying.

The child was really good at what he was doing. He seemed to judge well the strength of the wind and the movements of his kite. He appeared to know precisely when to let out more line and when to tighten up and how much. When he had fed out line until the kite was about as high as kites normally go, I noted the radiant satisfaction that shown in his face. And I was happy for him.

Then came a sudden thought: That kite stayed up there because that young man held that line firmly in his hand. Should the line be released or severed, the kite would be instantly out of control and would fall. Properly anchored, the April breeze bore it up and held it there; but in the absence of that anchorage, that same breeze would blow it, like a falling leaf, away.

As with that child's kite flying, so it is with our living. To stay up, a kite must be tied down; this is as true in our living as in kiting. Without anchorage, we are adrift, out of control, and subject to the whims of the winds. It is only as we are firmly tied to something worth being tied to that we are free to fly. Otherwise, we are blown about in the manner of autumn leaves in whirlwinds.

It is only as we are, somewhere near the center of life, truly committed to something sure and stable and lofty and good that we have the power to use the very winds that would otherwise bring us down or tear us apart. Only the well-grounded are fully free to fly.

OUR GO-AROUND TIMES

Several years ago, at age eight-two, a much loved and widely known scholar and author told me of an amusing and disconcerting experience that had been his and his family's many years before. With two small children, he and his wife were struggling to get started on the spectacular career that would be theirs.

One year, the couple had little money and none to spare for a costly vacation. So they decided to do something neither had ever done before—go on a camping vacation. Packing a tent and other equipment into their Baby Overland (remember that brand of car?), they went away to a favored New England destination.

Then came rain and more rain, a lot of rain. After several miserable days and nights, the couple stuffed all their water-sodden paraphernalia and their children into the small automobile and set out for home.

Night came. The rain was still falling, and as the night wore on the going became more and more difficult. Roads were mostly unpaved and marred by ruts, water puddles, and mud. Visibility was poor, auto head-lights dim, especially dim at slow speeds, and speeds were necessarily slow.

However, after hours of such difficulties, the roadway seemed to level out and become smooth. Speed could now be increased a little, and relief was felt both in the front and rear seats of the Overland. Mostly, this section of road was straight, with only a gentle curve every once in a while.

Soon, however, the driver became aware that none of the curves were right-handed ones; all went leftward, one after another, a dozen or so of them. Hey, wait a minute, thought the weary driver, this is impossible! Already greatly perplexed about the matter of curves, he then took note of another perplexing fact: Nowhere visible were any road signs or anything else normally seen near a highway.

At last, bringing the car to a stop, he got out and with a lighted lantern explored the surroundings—only to discover that in the darkness they had wandered onto a racetrack! Here they were circulating round and round and round but going nowhere.

I don't know if this story ever got into anything this prolific author ever wrote, but in my opinion it should have. And why? Because it suggests something important about life. Don't we, most of us at least, now and then come to our go-around times? We can be going and going but not really going anywhere. There may be a lot of activity, or maybe not, but nothing is really happening.

What can one do at such times? The answer, I think, is most clearly to be found in the story this friend told me. Having heard it I asked, "When you discovered yourselves on that racetrack, what did you do?" "The obvious," my friend replied, "we located a road that would go somewhere, got ourselves on it, and headed for home."

The Remains

Calling at a funeral home, I was met by the black-suited mortician, a rather morose and pompous fellow, who intoned, "Do you wish to see the remains?" By that, he meant to indicate the body of my aged friend that lay in an open casket at the farther end of the room.

Other than answer with a brief affirmative, I made no reply to the man. But I should have, and this is what I should have said:

"Remains? You call *this* remains? What you have on display in this casket, sir, is not what remains of my friend. What remains of him is not here. It is out there in the world that was his to live in. What remains of him is in the minds and hearts and memories of people whom he has touched along the way, people whom he has blessed by his kindness, people to whom, by his example, he has demonstrated the art of love.

"No, what you have here is not what remains of him. His remains are in the lives of little children who have looked up to him and drawn strength and courage and kindness from his face, who have read gentleness in his eyes, who have heard laughter in his voice. And, too, his remains are in the lives of folks he has helped and, by his helping, has inspired to help others.

"What remains of my friend, sir, you have not laid in this narrow aperture, nor can you. You cannot confine it here. It is out there on a hundred city streets, on many miles of country roads, around scores of family hearths, wherever the people are whom he has touched and blessed in his passing. And sir, something of my friend remains in me."

Growth Rings

Today I read the life story of a great oak tree. I read the story on a section crosscut from the tree's huge trunk. There the growth rings spoke to me of cold winters and hot summers and long dry spells the tree had lived through.

Through it all, for two centuries almost, the tree had stood strong through storms that wrenched its spreading limbs and sometimes tore the weaker ones away. It had stood some seasons in drought so withering that its glossy green leaves were faded and curled.

But it had stood, and it had lived, and it was yet living when it fell. Some of its roots having rotted away, and after the freezing and thawing of a long winter, it was brought down by the force of a mighty March wind.

As I studied those growth rings today, it was clear that for growing, some seasons had been more favorable than others. Broad bands and thin lines spoke of the changing times the tree had lived through.

I thought of my own life, these many years of it, and the seasons through which I, too, have lived. Unlike the tree, however, sometimes I have grown most when the growing was most difficult. Unlike the tree, I am not merely a product of circumstance, for in me there is transcending quality the tree never had.

My growth rings, like those of the tree, will show, nevertheless, that I too have come through cold winters, hot summers, and long dry spells of my own. Some of those rings will be broad, showing that in some seasons I grew a great deal; and other rings, I suppose, will be thin.

But now, here I am, living still; and I want to be yet living and growing when the winds of some faraway storm prove to be more than I can stand. When I go down, whatever else may be said, may it be known of me that I was still growing when I fell.

PASSING THE CANDY STORE

On a warm summer day on a busy city street, I overheard a mother say a remarkably instructive thing to her small son. Obviously, he was fretful, behaving badly; and obviously she was weary, but was exercising commendable self-control. As I passed them on the sidewalk, the child was tugging at his mother with one hand and with the other pointing and reaching toward the display in the window of a candy store.

It was only a small snippet of conversation that I heard—nothing of what the child said and only a single sentence from his mother. Taking a deep breath and sighing audibly, and with an air of patient exasperation, she said this: "Don't you *ever* get tired of wanting something?"

I've thought for years about that mother's question, and I find myself deeply impressed by it, for as I have observed our human scene, I think her question can have enormous relevancy in the lives of many people. Many of us, I suspect, have grown tired from carrying about with us a heavy burden of wanting. So many of us just can't pass the candy store without wanting some of everything that's there.

We are tired, many of us, and we don't know why. Ours is a vague sense of fatigue, a sort of subtle lassitude that settles on us like a fog. Usually we resolve that we will not surrender to it; so, perhaps with accelerated vigor, we keep going, keep doing.

However, in all of our going and doing we carry with us this burden that weighs us down. We want and we want and we want, and as soon as we get one thing we want another. We are never free from wanting; therefore, we have no concept of what our life would be like if we were.

In our modern world there is so much to be wanted—more than ever in history. The candy store is well supplied, the wares enticingly displayed. For most of us, it normally takes a lot of willpower to get past the candy store. One way to do it, of course, is to get past the appetite for candy. How can this be done? One good answer is: Just live a long time! Grow older, and all those trinkets that used to be so important don't matter so much anymore. What a feeling of freedom! It's so nice not to be wanting all those things!

But oh, pity those of that other generation who are half a century younger! Take heart, however, for in due time, they too will learn!

A Sense of Pilgrimage

Whoever loses a sense of pilgrimage is soon a vagabond. Moreover, without this sense, one is bereft of the major wellspring from which most courage flows.

What mighty motivation in 1620 empowered the men and women who dared the North Atlantic and braved the perils of Plymouth Plantation to endure the rigors and hardships of that awesome undertaking? Their governor, William Bradford, in his *Historie* probably put the answer best in five words: "They knew they were pilgrims."

As I have traced the trails of westward migration in America, I have looked almost disbelievingly upon the resolve, courage, and heroism of most of those people. Viewing wagon tracks in prairie sandstone and graves of those who perished along the way, I have found myself asking: What made them do it? Simply this, I think: They knew they were pilgrims.

But these are only overt illustrations of what it means to have a sense of pilgrimage. The profoundest meanings are not to be found in wagon tracks and monuments from another time and place, but within ourselves in our own time and circumstance.

We can go against heavy odds and endure awful hardships along the way if we can deeply feel that we are going somewhere. To be all we can be, we need a never-fading awareness that we are working our way onward to some distant goal; and the more elevated the destination the more noble the journey will be.

We are pilgrim creatures, we humans—all the way up from our caves and our cudgels. The spirit of pilgrimage is woven into the very fabric of what we are, and we deny ourselves an integral quality of our own nature if we quench this spirit or let it die.

However far we have come, there is somewhere yet to go; however high we have climbed, there are loftier heights yet to scale. If the goal is worthy, though we never reach it, we are the richer for having tried—for it is not so much the arrival as it is the struggle that makes us strong.

A Tooling of the Heart

The human spirit is like a factory or a refinery. It is forever receiving into it the raw materials of experience and circumstance, and it is forever making something of these and passing its product on.

A great factory has a receiving gate, an off-loading dock. At this entrance the raw materials flow in; by plane or truck or ship or train, in daily quotas they come. From most points of the compass, from distances near and far, the materials keep rolling in.

Like the factories of the industrial world, we human persons have our intake gates. They are busy; the traffic is heavy. It's impossible to know what will next be uncrated at our unloading docks. Sometimes, when we have ordered pleasure, circumstance delivers pain. Sometimes, when we expect it least, some unheralded messenger appears with something priceless. Our living is what we make of whatever comes.

An industrial plant also has an "out" gate, a shipping room, a loading dock. For the factory has an output; this is what factories are for. Using essentially the same materials, one will turn out automobiles, another will produce television receiving sets, and yet another will make paper clips or ballpoint pens. It all depends on what the factory is "tooled up" to do.

In our human lives we also have our output gates. We are exporters. Something is forever flowing out from our lives into the lives of others and into the world around us. What our output is to be will depend upon what we have "tooled up" to produce.

Some have inwardly equipped themselves to make something beautiful of everything that comes. Out of the most dismal of circumstance they produce the radiance of an inward peace and poise. From fragments of shattered hopes they mold new forms of beauty.

The human spirit has a remarkable productive power. All that enters it is processed, refined, and reformed into something of one kind or another. Of similar circumstance some make one thing and some make another. Sometimes only bitterness is spewed forth, or resentment, or hatred. It's a matter of tooling.

So let's tool up with gratitude and know that the world has been most blessed by its people who have taken their blessings, large or small, processed them through grateful hearts, and passed them on to others in deeds and words of love.

Let's tool up with courage, patience, self-control, and faith, and know that we can take our experiences, bright or dark, and of them make something beautiful. Blessed are they who do this early, and blessed is the world around them, for so they leave behind them as they go long, long trails of beauty, like tulips and daffodils standing tall beside the path. Later, to be sure, the path may be shorter, but do remember this: It's never too late for retooling.

Analogy for a Time of Trouble

The storm came in,
   borne on wings of raging wind,
And the sky was black,
   and the sun was hid.
But Father said, "Just wait—
   for this same wind
will take the storm away again."
And it did.

The Art of Measuring Mountains

Having spent most of my life in the eastern quarter of our country, I have long been impressed with the immensity of the American West. Everything is so big!

Once when traveling there, my family and I, we found ourselves driving not far from one of those majestic western mountains. Yonder on the horizon, its sloping sides swept up in graceful arcs; and there in the northern sky, its snow-capped summit melded with summer clouds. As the children talked about its beauty and its size, I said, 'Enjoy it while you can; we'll be out of sight of it in an hour or so."

But we weren't. How wrong I was! At the day's end we were still within clear view of that mountain. It was bigger than I had thought it was.

So it is with many of the great moments in our lives. We may come to them, observe them casually as we pass, and go on, not realizing how big and wonderful they really were.

They may tower in majestic splendor against the gray of our clouded sky, but we tend to go by and never really see. Later we may say, "Wasn't it beautiful there?" But somehow we missed it at the time.

How often we look back with nostalgic longing, trying to recapture a time long gone. Something calls it vaguely to mind, and we reach for it, as though to seize it and hold it and live it again. We yearn so much to taste the sweet nectars we had mostly missed before.

We had hurried by, and now we remember just enough to let us know that there was more. As we see it now, it should have been a mountain peak of joy, but somehow we must have missed it then.

Oh, if we might enjoy our mountains as we pass them! But we are so busy, so preoccupied, so involved that many times we don't. Instead, we look back later and say: I think I missed something there. And we wonder how great those mountains really were.

If only we might feel the upward pull of summits at those times when the summits are actually pulling! If only at the time we might turn loose our souls and let them soar! If only we might live our mountains when it's mountain time! How often, however, it is only with the passing of the years that we begin to realize how big and beautiful our mountains must have been.

My Treasure Chest

I have this marvelous old treasure chest, gold-banded, jewel-studded, and made secure against any who might pilfer there. It is mine alone, and only I have a key. Most of the time it is locked, but I open it up now and then that I might delight again in some memento from another time.

I have been for a long while stowing away in it things I have wanted to keep. But every once in a while, as I go through it, I come upon something I wonder about and find myself saying, "Now why did I ever keep that? I should have tossed it aside long ago." Lest I clutter it up with junk, I've tried always to put only worthwhile stuff into my chest; but I fear that from time to time some of the junk did get in.

Mostly, however, the things I have are things I really cherish. Here in this chest I have kept and treasured what I've loved. All of it is still there, much of it as fresh as yesterday. Some is rather finger-marked from my much handling over the years. Often, when I have been lonely or weary or troubled in spirit, I have gone into my treasures and have found consolation and inspiration there.

Usually I have only to crack the lid a little to find something that brings me joy. Although some things there are quite old, others are somewhat new, for until this very moment I have kept adding others. Now, after this long while, my chest is so well filled I can barely close the lid.

This marvelous chest of mine—do you perhaps wonder about it? Well, it's my memory. You also have one, you know.

These chests of ours—how very precious to us their contents can be!

Moreover, the good news is that the longer we live, the more of these treasures we have. The years may rob us of other things, but until memory itself begins to fail, time keeps adding treasures. If over the passing years we treasure up the happy things, how rich is the treasury we have at last! It is pleasant now and then to open the lid, pluck out a precious thing, hold it up to the light, fondle it a little, and enjoy it all over again.

Part III

Our Call to the Mountain

It's a remarkable story from an ancient time. Moses and his Israelites were out of Egypt but not yet in Canaan; their situation was precarious. These thousands were now encamped in a valley at the base of a mountain called Sinai. Here, one day, God spoke to Moses, saying, "Hew two tablets of stone and I will write upon them; be ready in the morning and come up into the mountain."

That night, with hammer and chisel, the man Moses worked upon the stones, chipped and shaped them with consummate care. With dawn's first light he was ready. He took the stones, smooth-hewn, and climbed into the mists and mystery of Sinai. Somewhere up there, in some way, Moses and God met; and when the man came down, the tablets he carried bore engraved upon them the Ten Commandments by which we of humankind were enjoined to live.

There is a voice that still speaks—call it God or Reality—and it speaks to all of us. The voice is saying: You prepare your tablets, and I will write upon them.

Today the voice says: You bring me the raw materials of your life, and I will touch and change and refine them for you; you make ready the seedbed, and I will produce the growth; you open the door, and I will come in. Someone is forever saying to us: Prepare the tablets of your life for the moving finger of God.

So, if you make in your heart large places for understanding, compassion, and love, they will come. If you stretch the rooms of our soul with thankfulness, generosity, and self-control, beauty will move in and abide. If you open your mind to insight and truth, these too will come.

So prepare your tablets, shape them well, hone them smooth, and be ready in the morning. No, you don't know when your morning will come, but it will. When it comes, your call to the mountain will also come. That will be the great day of your opportunity and testing.

The most thrilling chapters of history have been written by persons who were prepared when the great moment came; when, their tablets finely finished and ready, they have met Life and Life's God in the mystic recesses of some thundering summit. The voice of Life still speaks to every one of us: Prepare yourself for the mountain, and be ready when your morning comes.

Mountains and mornings! Over many years, there will be many; and of these, the final will be the finest.

Anchors and Sails

Wind-driven ships must be equipped with both sails and anchors. The sails are for going forward, and the anchors are for holding steady. There are times for unfurling sails, and there are times for dropping anchors, and the good sailor must know the times.

How great is the thrill to see a tall ship on a clear day, her white sails billowed by the push of soft wind, her graceful prow knifing silently into the rolling swell! But it is not always so. There come the winds of storm and the great salt waves, and furious fingers tear at every jib and spar; the sun is hid, and there is one darkness blending sea and sky; the sails are reefed, the anchors cast, and all hands stand by; and somewhere in the deeps the anchor flukes have keyed themselves to the ocean floor, and there they hold.

So it is with our life; and thanks to its master design, our life's seafaring craft is equipped with sails for going on when we can and with anchors for holding when we must.

How exhilarating to feel the vibrant surge when life is under full sail! Things are going well, our seas are right for sailing, the winds are with us, our skies are clear, and our compass needle lies steady to the pole.

However, it isn't always so. Comes at length an anchor time; it's a storm, or the voyage is done, and now the anchors are cast. How reassuring to know that deep beneath all surface turbulence the anchors hold secure. Though wind and wave and tide can bring our craft up tight against the chains, she firmly stands, awaiting another fair and sunny day.

My Heart Has Been a Passing Place

My heart has been a passing place,
  Fragile soil pressed by varied feet
Coming and going,
  Some lightly dancing though,
Some plodding in bruising boots,
  All leaving tracks.

I planted a garden;
  But sorrow came and tramped my roses down.
I laid a cobbled path for beauty;
  Cleated heels tore my cobbles up.

I remember most the dancers,
  Elfin figures on elfin feet,
Scattering stardust as they came,
  Leaving sweet aromas when they went.

Our Diminishing Alternatives

In all its scores of years, one's life is an ongoing process of diminishing alternatives. As we start out, there's an option in almost every direction we turn. Along the way, we can choose among many roads, merging and diverging as they do across the landscape of our years.

But the farther we go, the fewer of these there are. Out there somewhere is a very narrow place to which we will one day come, a narrow passage we will all go through.

Early on, we have, for instance, options of education, occupation, lifestyle. As our journey continues, courses are charted, ways are chosen; and the farther we go along any road, the fewer roads there are that diverge from it.

Early in our life, health is normally not a limitation and energy abounds; but later, energies ebb and limitations begin to build their fences around us. Little by little, year by year, our list of possibilities gets shorter and shorter; we must give up this and that, and we find that our range of activity is irrepressibly closing in around us.

Infirmities increase; then illness comes and shuts us in. We look for a way out but can find none. It's a one-way road from here on, and the road is narrow. We have virtually used up all our options. At last we arrive at that place where a solitary necessity crowds all our options out, and there is no alternative.

What morbid prospects, you say! Oh no, not at all; it's marvelous, really. For if along the way we choose our options well, the diminishing alternatives serve simply to set a focus on the ultimate fulfillment of it all. Assuming that we work our way forward discreetly, as alternatives narrow life broadens until at length, when the alternatives come to zero, life reaches infinity—the goal to which it had aspired from the start.

Perspective from 2069

Once there was the sky—
Blue, they say it was—
    and stars
    that could be seen with natural human eye.
On Earth the land was green,
    and in valleys cool clean waters ran.
Mountaintops were capped with snow.
All of this, it is said, was not so very long ago—
    in the golden-time of Man,
    before the firestorm came
    and the deep, dark gray.
I do not know,
    for I myself have never seen a star.

But an old man is here—
    how old nobody knows, not even he—
    who sits most time by the cavern fire;
    and when the mood is on him
He talks,
    speaking always of time that used to be.
His moods most often come
    at intervals when the deeper darkness falls,
And always he begins by saying,
    "Well, the sun must be setting now..."
What that saying means
    we do not really know.

Managing Our Memories

Were we to speak about managing a million dollars, some would have no interest, because not everyone has that amount of money. Here, however, we speak about managing our memories, and almost everybody has one of these.

Memories are composed of three ingredients, mixed in various proportions and to various consistencies. In most memories there is some of the good, some of the bad, and some of the indifferent, with the indifferent in greatest abundance and of least significance.

It is with the good and the bad in memory that we are most concerned. What we hold in memory is crucial to our state of happiness and sense of well-being and is quite influential in the establishment of attitudes, perspectives, and priorities. It should be obvious that good memories are more to be desired than bad ones, so let us observe three things about the management of memory.

First: Practice remembering the right things. Of course, we cannot normally obliterate an unpleasant memory by moving a pleasant one up front and keeping it there, but doing so will really move us a long way in that direction. So, dwell on the good, relive it, savor it, enjoy it. Be selective of the thoughts you entertain; we can be, you know. We cannot prevent unwelcome thoughts from sometimes flying like birds through our minds, but by entertaining better thoughts, we can keep the unwelcome ones from roosting there. It's a good idea to provide roosting places for the better birds!

Second: Practice forgetting the things that ought to be forgotten. Those petty hurts, the slights and insults, the bruises and abrasions suffered long since—these tend to fasten themselves like parasites upon us and suck our life away. Mind space is too precious to be taken up by seething cauldrons of resentment or bitterness. Much of life energy is drained off by hanging tenaciously onto what should be turned loose.

Third: Practice remembering the right things at the right times. We give ourselves an important advantage if we can call up from the past that which will help us most at some crucial present moment. Confronting hard decisions or powerful temptations, it's important what we remember then. How often, if we but train our minds to do it when we are pressured, harried, or pestered, we can retreat for refuge into a pleasant memory, finding solace and inspiration there.

Some disciplines are difficult; they impose unpleasant requirements upon us. It's not so with this one; the exercise is pleasant and agreeable.

Essentially, it's a simple matter. Make indelible the great experiences, the better moments; make mountaintop times as unforgettable as possible; firmly seize and hold the finest thoughts that ever come. Whatever in memory is affirmative, dwell on this, move it upstage and center, and keep it there. Keep your spotlight on it, and let your whole being applaud its presence and performance.

THE WORLD WITHIN

We live in a wonderful world! Circling the sun, the planet's seasons change; spinning on angled axis, the Earth weaves her tapestry of day and night. Lights and shadows, sunshine and rain, sowing time and harvest, continuing yet ever changing, the world moves on. Generations come; generations go: There is birth and life, growth, and age, and living things that number in the millions.

We can look to the horizons, seeing sunset and dawn. We can lift our eyes to the stars and ponder the galaxies, the depth of space, the mystery and marvel of light. We can experience the beauty of a rose, the fragrance of lilac, or the aroma of moss on a mountain rock. We can hear bird songs and winds and falling rain and the voices of a thousand creatures that speak in tongues all their own. There are the mighty mountains and the seas, and jungles and plains and fields of growing grain.

We can direct our gaze across the earth and take in the marvelous products of human genius: great cities, structures, machines, and ships that sail Earth's seas and others that probe remotest space.

Yes, it's out there, the wonderful world we live in. We can travel to see it; we can reach to touch it. It's out there, around us everywhere.

But there is another world. This is the world within, the world of what we *are*. This is the inward world of feeling and longing, of hungering and reaching and seeking. It is the world of joy and sorrow, of pleasure and pain. It is the world where deep currents of emotion run, where tides of aspiration flow, where exists or has existed all the love that is or ever was.

Think of all that happens in this inner world in a lifetime of years. First comes the rose-tinted glow of childhood, with fairies and fancies; there is the slow dawning of awareness and growing pains, and a lot of laughter and a lot of tears. Comes then the romance of early adulthood, the quest for identity, the adventure of discovery, the realization of love. There is then the long trek through the creative years, with choices to be made, burdens to be carried, work to be done, hard roads to be traveled, rugged mountains to be climbed, and along the way some sun-kissed summits to be enjoyed.

Then there is advanced age, when all values are seen more clearly in the light of accumulated time. Think of it: all the hopes and dreams, all the anxieties and fears, all the crisscross of lights and shadows that come with the passing years.

Yes, it's a wonderful world, this world within. It's most wonderful, however, for its infinite capacity to be radiantly bright and beautiful, and our finest privilege is to make it so. By a lifetime of attitude and action, the world within is at length formed and colored. Over a long span of years the process goes on. Other abilities can change with time. Here, however, is a power each of us has to our very last day—the power of adding somewhat more of brightness and beauty to this wonderful world within. It's never too late for this.

Tethers and Polestars

If I were able to speak with every young person who stands at life's starting line, here is one very important thing I'd like to say:

First, find out what you believe; lay hold of something you can believe in. Be sure it's a truth, an important and positive truth, and the greater the truth the better. Seize that truth and hold it consciously and firmly.

Wherever you may later be, let this truth be your reference point. Find your way with it as your guiding star, and allow nothing to eclipse it from your view.

Yonder above Earth's north pole stands Polaris, the only fixed star in our sky. It is commonly called the polestar, and sailors have long guided their vessels by it. As you begin your life's voyage, find your Polaris, get a fix on your polestar, and then steer by it. For the conscientious, that star can be honesty; for the noble, it can be purity; for the Christian, it can be Christ. Whatever it is for you, fix upon it and never let it go.

You will need, you see, a principle to live by. One stands in a slippery place who has no principle to stand on. And, of course, one can get terribly lost who has no star to steer by.

You will need, as we all do, a tether stake to tie to. Farm animals are sometimes tethered to keep them from wandering away. Lest we wander, you and I need our tetherings, too. To be tethered is to be firmly centered on something worthy: a good idea, a noble aim, a great ideal. Some people tether themselves to small notions with short ropes, and the limited range becomes almost a prison. Let it not be so with you. Understand that if we have a fixed center, our circumferences can vary widely and range far. That person is best prepared and qualified for living who is well tethered, but with a long rope.

A star to steer by and a tether stake to tie to—these are two images of one great truth: You need as you go a philosophy of life—a clear perception of what life is and means and of what *your* life can be and mean to you.

Long ago a great man wrote, "For me to live is …" That man had conviction. What is yours? You fill in the blank. Lay hold of the greatest truth you can find. Then you will be ready to go.

The Journey Home

There's an old song: "Lord, I'm Coming Home."
   Well, I am, Lord.
   I'm on my way.
I don't know just when I'll get there, Lord.
   There'll probably be some detours along the way,
   and there'll be things I'll have to do in passing.
I may have to stop and work at the factory a decade or two,
   or maybe more,
   or at the office or the store, I don't know.
I may come by way of a marriage altar
   and take the hand of someone to walk with as I come
And, too, I may spend some years at a little white cottage,
   playing with some children that I'll be loving
   and watching grow.
But, Lord, I'm on my way. I'm coming home.
It may be a long, long road, and rough and steep in places,
   and by the time I get there
   I may be tottering on feeble feet and walking slow
   from the rigors of the journey and the time it took.
But, Lord, all the while, I'll be coming home.

God Knows When the Water Is Rising

In South America, a huge dam was constructed across a valley, forming one of the world's great man-made lakes. When the construction work was finished and the gates closed, the water gradually rose. In the process of flooding the valley, many islands were formed. Some of these were temporary, becoming smaller and smaller as the water level climbed, until eventually they disappeared completely.

On these pinnacles of land, wild animals of the jungle took refuge from the rising water. If these were not rescued and taken to the mainland, they perished as the islands were overflowed.

Kind persons organized to save the stranded creatures. The rescuers assembled a small fleet of motorboats, and, equipped with ropes, snares, nets, and cages, they went forth on their missions of mercy.

But the wild creatures resisted capture and, if captured, often fought their captors to the point of exhaustion. Some of the more powerful and skillful eluded their rescuers or, if brought into captivity, managed to escape. Many swam away into the rising water and were lost.

The poor creatures were afraid to trust the people who had come to save them. In their superior wisdom, the rescuers knew what was best, but in their limited range of knowledge and experience, the animals were unable to understand.

So it is, I am sure, in the ways God deals with me. I'm sure God understands a great deal that is mysterious and strange to me. However things may appear at the time, I hope I may always remember that in every circumstance God intends only good for me. When things are unclear and I am unable to understand, I am resolved to trust God more.

At times when I think I am secure and safe on my small island and something comes along to nudge me off, it may very well be because God knows the water is rising.

THE ART OF LOSING VICTORIOUSLY

There is much more failure in the world than there is success. Ten young runners are on the starting line. Bodies poised, eyes on the goal, they await the starting gun. All want to win, but nine will lose.

A roll call of dreams would reveal that far more are never fulfilled than ever are. I suppose this means that we should be prepared to see our dreams go by in default and their fulfillments never come. I remain convinced, however, that it is good to believe we can win, to foretaste the winner's applause. Believing helps to get us up and going.

But what if we don't win? Are we ready for this? The athletic commissioner of our state recently pointed out that many high school students do not know how to act when the team loses. He said, "I wish sometime someone would explain to the student body that someone is going to lose."

Many of us are not inwardly equipped to deal with anything but victory. In the struggle to achieve or in the battle for health, we often have difficulty being good losers. We need a philosophy for times when we cannot win. What might such a philosophy be? Let's say just four things about it:

1. It would realistically accept failure as a fact of life. Things will not always work out in first-choice ways. Even the most successful person sometimes fails. No one will win every race; everyone will taste defeat of some kind sometime.

2. It would be ready to say: If I have done my best and could not succeed, this is all that is required of me, and this I all I should require of myself. There is something worse than failure; it is not to try. It was Cicero who said, "If you aspire to the highest place, it is no disgrace to stop at second or even third."

3. It would recognize that failure at one point does not mean failure at all points. Whatever may go down in failure, the rest of life still remains intact. One is never a failure simply because he or she has failed; failure and success can coexist within the human experience at any given time. If we look only at our failures, we are not seeing the whole of our life. We must not permit a view of our defeats to obscure our perception of everything else.

4. It would have us always, in any instance of failure, look for the good that is bigger than the failure. That good is always there, the ground of a new hope.

Having a life view such as this, we can be victorious in defeat. Seeing life and effort in this light, we understand that in many instances there is no higher achievement than simply to do the very best we can. Having done that, whatever the outcome, we have not gone down in defeat, but can stand tall, aglow with victory. Real victory in life is not to win over all others, but to rise to our own best.

BRIGHT BLUE AND GOLD

I gave my child a ball of twine
   And put him to play upon the floor.
Then I sat an watched this child of mine
   As many times I had watched before.

With eager reach of dimpled hands
   He fondly grasped his fluffy prize,
Bright blue and gold with twisted strands,
   A delight for childhood eyes.

Then, all absorbed in his own small world,
   He began to unwind the ball;
And the twine was tossed and twisted and twirled
   With no care or plan at all.

He laughed and leaped and rolled,
   And the loops grew large and wild
Until he was all enmeshed in blue and gold—
   I could scarcely see the child!

After a while, and all worn out,
   He lapsed exhausted on the floor;
He plucked at the strands that wrapped him about,
   But they tangled more and more.

Then, lifting his face, his eyes sought mine;
   With anxious look and a frantic plea,
His voice half prayer and the other half whine,
   He said, "Daddy, please untangle me."

And I thought as I knelt beside him there
   How very much I am like him:
Receiving bright blues and golds from everywhere,
   I often so badly tangle them.

I take from life's spindle the brilliant strands
   To pattern and weave this life of mine;
Then somehow strangely in my bungling hands
   I have only a mass of tangled twine.

I find myself all wrapped about
   With the galling coils I cannot unbind—
All tied and tortured within, without,
   And troubled in heart and mind.

Shackled and trammeled and sore distressed,
   And wanting so much to be free,
I lift my face in desperate quest
   And say, "Father, please untangle me."

Lights for Darkened Windows

Samuel was a kind, gentle, grandfatherly type of man who had taught art long past the usual retirement age. The beautiful young woman he had married at twenty-four had been taken from him in a tragic accident only two years later. Then for forty-three years he had faithfully and joyfully devoted himself to students in landscape and still-life painting. In this he had been preeminently successful, especially so if success be measured by the degree of adoration and respect accorded.

His success, though, had reached far beyond the art of painting. Thoughtful neighbors had long ago discovered that merely to observe the man became an object lesson in the art of living. In his tender way of touching others, he had brought much joy into the lives of those around him. Many who had walked in dark valleys of distress had found their way out, guided by the light of his encouragement and example. Among those who knew him well, he gradually became known as Father Sam.

One day not long ago, Father Sam was working with a class, going about among the students, observing their work. Marilyn had just finished hers—an autumn scene, a clouded day. Among large elm trees, a narrow trail curved up to an ancient turreted house that stood stark and dark atop a hill. With palette and brush still in hand, Marilyn stood back a little in quizzical appraisal of the work she had done.

Father Sam approached, joining her there, studying with her the canvas before them. After a few moments, he gestured to the nearby container of bright yellow paint and quietly said, "Your windows, Marilyn, your windows."

With that kind of luminous smile that can sometimes come with sudden happiness, Father Sam's pupil dipped her brush and deftly put lights in the windows of that forlorn and darkened house. In that instant the entire scene was brilliantly transformed.

Learning of this classroom episode, I thought: For many years, Father Sam has been doing just this for countless people he has touched along his way. This man has spent his life putting lights in darkened windows.

Then came a second thought: what finer memorial can one ever leave behind than a string of lights in windows that once were dark and desolate.

From my heart arose this prayer: Help me, Lord, please help me in all my remaining time, wherever there is darkness, whenever I can, to add some touch of light.

Delayed Revelations

From a lesser road, you approach a major interstate highway, and the entrance ramp is just ahead. Road signs will let you know which direction you will be going and to what city, but there is no sign telling you how many miles to get there. This will appear later, probably when you are some distance down the road.

Have you noticed that our system of superhighways is so designed that it is only sometime after you have committed yourself that you find out how far you have to go? I have to wonder: Was the system designed to work this way because this is the way life works? Probably not; but this is indeed the way life works: first the commitment; then the cost of it.

For instance, two stand at the altar of marriage and commit themselves, each to the other; but it is only sometime afterward that they will discover all that their commitment involves. Later these two may commit themselves to parenthood, but many years will go by before they know all that lies before them down the road.

Let us be thankful, however, that some revelations are of the delayed kind. I'm sure that many times we would never start if we knew in advance how long or arduous our journey would be. So, it seems there is built into our human system a mechanism to get us started and keep us going. This mechanism is called commitment. Without it, the world would have much less adventure and achievement in it and much more of the boring and inconsequential.

Commitment means direction, purpose, destination; it takes one beyond mere day-to-day existence and puts one on the road that goes somewhere—somewhere worth going, one supposes. If the road is sometimes rough, the truly committed will see it through. Unlike the proverbial kamikaze pilot who flew thirteen missions, the truly committed are—well, truly committed!

The uncommitted may "get along," but the committed go somewhere, and there's adventure in that. So—that entrance ramp just ahead? Take it!

Need I Go It Alone?

Our son, when a very small child, was a quite independent and self-sufficient sort. Resisting help, he insisted on figuring things out for himself and doing them on his own.

However, about the eighth or tenth word he learned to say was the word *trouble*, pronouncing that single word as though saying, "I've at last run into a situation I can't handle, and I need help." Anyway, his mother and I soon learned that when we heard that word, the child was ready to be helped.

Once, I remember, he had caught a foot between the slats of his playpen and was unable to dislodge it. Another time, playing with blocks, he had tried frantically and at length to put the right block in the wrong hole or to do something similar.

Whatever the problem, when the little fellow could at last admit that he had run into something he was unable to manage, he was willing to call for help—and *accept* it. This is the point—*accept* it. Much as we may have wanted to help him, our son seemed to feel most of the time that he didn't need our help and was therefore unready to receive it.

I wonder if God doesn't sometimes see us as being somewhat that way. We try to go it alone, as through God were not there. When the Divine hand tries to reach over our shoulder to guide our fumbling hands a little, we are so prone to push it aside. With most of us, it's only when we run into something we can't muddle through or when we have so badly tangled things that we cannot untangle them at all, that we are willing to let God help us.

Knowing so well what our needs and limitations are and wanting so much to assist us with help, God is no doubt sorely distressed that we are so unwilling to accept it. I wonder if God may spend much time waiting to hear us pronounce that simple, prayerful word "Trouble!"

As his mother and I always stood ready to help our son, so does God stand ready to help us. Why are we so slow to acknowledge that we need the help that God can give? We readily accept the aid of the banker or the druggist or the plumber, and are quite willing even to pay for it. God's aid is offered without price, and yet we often spurn it, usually feeling that we do not need it.

God offers guidance for our forward journey, but we rely so much on the evening news or the latest social commentary. God offers a peace that "passes understanding," but how desperately we seek our peace everywhere else. God offers the forgiveness of our sins, but we seem most times to believe we can get along without that forgiveness. As we grope our way through life, God offers us a guiding and helping hand that we are so strangely unwilling to take. In our vain unwillingness to admit our need of help, how much we deny ourselves, how very much we miss.

THE PARTING: A FAREWELL TO LIFE

Good companions we, traveling together far—
   I salute you, cherished friend!
Yonder lies the road by which we came;
   From this hilltop
I see it stretching there
   Across the landscape of all our yesterdays,
Winding out of dimness beyond the reach of sight,
   Looping through the foothills,
Ever climbing, and broader as it nears,
   Its shadowed parts and brighter places
Blending into one
   Beneath the twilight rays
From the great descending sun.
   Enthralled, I walked this way with you;
Though at first a stranger, so I thought,
   I came to know you well,
And you were good to me.
   Besides, you caressed me with your joy;
Sometimes you let me feel you pain,
   But ever to sense the wonder of what you are.
Knew I from the start the journey would bring us here?
   That here would be our parting-place,
This our parting-time?
   I knew, I think, that sometime, somewhere it must be,
But I gave it little place in thought.
   Now I must let you go;
From here I go alone.
   Or may it be that I will reach
To clasp another hand?
   Our ways diverge;
I must go on, and so, I think, must you.
   Farewell, good friend, goodbye.
In parting, however, I beg you tell me this:
   Will we meet again?

The Miracle That Is Memory

You are traveling through a beautiful and fertile land. The roadsides are alive with color, flowers everywhere in bloom, bowing and waving as gentle summer breezes tiptoe softly by. Delectable fruits grow on nearby trees, all ripe for the plucking. Still waters mirror the wild woodlands that line the shore, and beyond, on shaded hillsides, sparkling rivulets murmur their ways toward a distant sea. Above, the sky is blue, broken only by white accents artfully arranged here and there. How very delightful is it all!

However, traveler that you are, you must pass on by. You must, for you have duties to do and night will fall. Going away from all this that you have seen, you wish that you might take it with you.

Well, you can—for I speak of a mile or so on your journey of life—and you have a remarkable capability called memory. Because of this, you don't have to leave everything behind as you pass; in a very real way, you can take it with you.

By means of memory we can keep and treasure what is precious. However dismal the day, we can adorn it with bright portraits of yesterday's golden glow. A lovely song says, "I memorize moments"; how wonderful that we can!

Consider how memory serves us. Looking back, we can reach back, and reaching back, we can lay hold of some cherished instant of time and bring it up to now and give it life again. How can this miracle occur? The answer lies in an understanding of three simple words:

Remember. Re-member. The word means to "member again." In buildings constructed of wood or steel, we speak of frame "members": sills, rafters, joists. When we construct a framed building, we "member" it. If we disassemble it, perhaps move it to another location and reassemble it, we are "re-membering" it. To remember an event from the past, then, is to reassemble that event in the mind. It is to take the elements of that past event and, in the mind, put them together again, there to have them re-exist as the re-membered structure from time gone by.

Recollect. Re-collect. To collect things is to bring them together, to assemble them in relationship one with another. To re-collect is to do this again. To recollect the past is to do just this, to reach back into the yesterdays, bring forward what once was there, and in the mind let it be—again.

Recall. Re-call. To call is to shout an appeal, to give a summons, to say "come." To recover a precious moment of time-gone-by we turn to the past, and we call that moment back from the yesterdays into which it has gone. We bring it up to now, and in the mind it lives again.

Memory is one of life's finer gifts. Especially privileged are we who have accumulated a great storehouse of pleasant memories to enjoy, and if every now and then an unpleasant one tries to intrude, we can always send an army of pleasant ones to chase it away.

THE EXPECTANT PAUSE

My office was next door to the house where I and my family lived, and a window overlooked the lawn. One summer day when our son was a wee lad, his mother told him to go out into the yard and call me to lunch. Through my open window, I heard his call: "Daddy! Daddy! Daddy! Daddy!" —one "daddy" after another, with no interval between the "daddies." He continued screeching that word as loudly and rapidly as he could.

Immediately upon hearing the first call, I answered, and I continued to answer. But he continued to call, and because he kept on calling, he was unable to hear my response.

At last I left my room, went down a corridor, out a side door, and approached my son in the yard. As he and I walked together into the house, I said to him, "Son, when you call me, stop every once in a while and listen for me to answer."

Suddenly I realized that perhaps I had said to him something God might want to say to me. How many times have I screamed at God, wondering why God wouldn't answer, while all along he wanted me just to get still long enough listen? I concluded then that when I pray to God I must leave some room for God to get an answer in.

When I pray, have I any hope that God will answer me? Not much is evident unless occasionally I pause and listen. I can express my *wishes* by many words or frantic motions, but it is by the attentive pause that I express my *faith*.

A TIME FOR SMILING

Professor Collins was retired when I knew him. He had served with distinction on the faculties of two or three universities and as the president of a Midwestern college. He was a man of quiet dignity and immense personal strength, erudite and finely tuned, with an extraordinary fund of knowledge and a doctoral degree in philosophy.

One evening, so this scholarly gentleman told me, it was his role to spend a couple of hours alone with his three-year-old grandson. One of his grandfatherly duties that evening was to get the little one tucked into bed. So, with the child on his lap, he helped his grandson with his bedtime devotions.

The small one launched heartily into his memorized prayer. The first few words came freely; then there was hesitation, followed by two or three words uncertainly spoken. Unable to remember the rest of the prayer, his voice trailing off at last to a total stop, the child lifted his sleepy eyes to his grandfather's face and said plaintively, "Granddaddy, I stuck."

Telling me of this, Dr. Collins said, "You know what I did? I said to my little grandson, 'That's all right; I understand. Sometimes granddaddy gets stuck too. I'll help you, and together we'll see if we can get through your prayer.'" Then Dr. Collins said to me, "And don't you know, *together we did!*"

Now see this picture with me—with pleasure, please: an elderly, scholarly gentleman and a simple, trusting child together in prayer—in the process of getting unstuck! I suspect that as he looked in upon those two that night, God smiled.

Part IV

SEEING THE PICTURE WHOLE

A landscape artist, painting, does not always stand at an arm's length from his canvas. He must not limit his attention to the isolated details of what he is doing. Occasionally he steps back to view his work from a distance. He needs to see how his thousands of brush-stokes fit together to produce an overall result.

Likewise, our perspective on life is much improved if sometimes we can step back and see it whole. We can become so occupied with its daily brush-stokes that we have no real perception of the whole scene we are painting on the canvas of the ongoing years. Our attentions can be so consumed by the requirements of daily living that we have little awareness of the dimensions and directions of life itself.

So, occasionally we need to step back from the canvas and try to see the picture whole. A stroke here or there, the colors we've used, the lights and shadows we've painted in—what does it all come out to be? What should we do now? What additional colors do we need? What strokes complete the art we commenced so long ago?

Here we look beyond the varied episodes of our daily doings and see the glory of it all. We look beyond the brush-strokes that make the art so that we might view the art the brush-stokes have made—and are making.

Of course, it is only as colors and contours are applied with care that the resulting work can merit a place among the masters. When the picture is done, however, it will not be the individual brush-strokes that a viewer will see, but the completed scene. Ultimately, it will be this that matters most.

The Best of All Invitations

I have been at various times invited by fine people to nice places for exciting and important occasions. But no invitation have I ever prized more highly than one that came by relay to me from a long time ago. It's a three-word invitation from God: "Come unto me."

Some have cherished invitations to the White House, or to opening night at the Met, or to the coronation of a British queen. But none of those invitations meant more to those people than this invitation has meant to me.

Once I was invited to party, only to discover that a fellow wanted me there in order to sell me a set of books. On another occasion, I was invited to spend a couple of days at a lakeside hideaway in the hills, but there was a hook in it, a catch: some real estate people wanted me to buy one of the building lots they were trying to sell.

But there's no catch to it when the Lord says, "Come." The Lord has no ulterior motive; he wants me for who I am and for all that I can become; he wants me not for his sake, but for mine. Being human, I want to be wanted; I need to feel that I matter to somebody, that I have some significance somehow. Well, in this regard, no invitation ever helped me more.

Tomorrow's mail may bring many invitations and the telephone many more, but I know this: Whatever invitations may come, none will ever surpass this one, so graciously given, offering so much, saying so simply, "Come."

Moreover, I have this to be thankful for: Should I never hereafter receive another invitation from anybody, this one is "standing," and I will always have it. Others may omit me from their guest lists, but God never will.

A Victory Within

Many years ago, as a student in Boston I walked almost daily up and down the side of Beacon Hill, between Mount Vernon Street and North Station. Normally, my route took me along Joy Street, and Joy was not the most joyful of Boston's streets. Once a nice area, it had become a slum—dirty, littered, unkempt, a haven of derelicts.

One warm spring morning as I climbed the hill, scarcely able to bear the stench that assailed me from all sides, I heard singing from somewhere up ahead. Rounding a corner, I came upon a group of men loading a garbage truck. As he picked up the cans and dumped them, one of the men was singing! He was an African American with a big smile and a singing voice that was really quite good.

He was really going at it, both his working and his singing. You'd never guess what that fellow was singing— "My Blue Heaven"! You know, that Walter Donaldson/George Whiting number: "Just Mollie and me and baby makes three, and we're happy in my blue heaven."

Continuing up the hill to my classes, I was sure that here was an utterly unbeatable man. I thought: There's no way you can defeat a man who can sing like that in a place like this. He wasn't singing because someone compelled him to, but because a song was in him and just had to come out.

I think a victory was built into the man; it was already there. He had put it there, and it was well established there. Any assailant who would ever try to undo him would have to deal with that victory first. I don't think any defeat could ever touch it!

LAUNCHINGS UNLIMITED

The coming of the Pilgrims from England to America is a story well known by almost everyone. Not so well known, however, is the fact that before they sailed for this continent, these people had spent several years as refugees in Holland. From Leiden, in that country, they crossed the Channel to England, where they boarded the ship Mayflower for their voyage to the New World.

Their pastor was John Robinson, and their final Sunday in Holland was a historic experience for this pastor and these people. The pastor identified the occasion as such a time, and in his message of the day he rose to heights both inspiring and prophetic.

From the pulpit that day, Robinson saw beyond the immediate circumstance and said something of much meaning for all people in all time. This, or something very similar to this, is what Robinson said to his assembled congregation: "Every assembly is a time filled with destiny. Every Sunday men and women go forth from their tryst with God to face nameless responsibilities. Before the week is out, some may have launched their Mayflower and embraced a God-given adventure."

This is so true, isn't it? We never know, do we? Never on any Sunday, nor on any other day, can you or I know what Mayflowers we may be called upon to launch before another week goes by—or another day.

Therefore, whether by the week or day by day, we are well advised to keep ourselves ready for whatever launchings there may be, for whatever new seas we may be called upon to sail, for whatever new shores we may touch before the voyage is done: Awakening with any dawn, we may find that some new Mayflower, expected or unexpected, has silently slipped into our port. There she stands, her gangplank in place and the wind already in her sails.

Prelude for a New Beginning

Did you ever try to put an active, small boy to bed? Evening has come, and the little fellow has had a busy day. He's tired, so very, very tired, but he isn't through playing yet. There's just one more thing he wants to do, maybe two. He'll probably tell you in half a dozen ways that going to bed will spoil all his fun. He can say, as many small boys have said, "If I have to go to bed, it will be the end of everything."

But at last he is persuaded—or forced—and to bed he goes. Almost at once he is asleep, and all the king's horses couldn't awaken him! Not until morning.

Ah! Morning! A fresh new boy tumbles out of bed, new stars in his eyes, to begin a fresh new day. Immediately, he has myriad ideas of interesting things to do—or get into!

After all, the coming of night was not the end. He thought so at the time. But the night really came with a soothing touch of blessing to put vigor into a tired little boy and replace the whine of fatigue with the glad hum of happiness.

But the little fellow doesn't seem to remember, for tonight it will be just as hard to get him into bed as it was a night ago. And again he'll be telling you that going to bed will absolutely be the end of everything.

Well, aren't we all just grown-up children? We grow older with the passing years, and the night of time settles around us. We are tired, and the necessity of dying is upon us. Coming to this time, how often we say: It's the end of everything! But it isn't. There has never yet fallen a night that has not been followed by the light of a new day.

We know it's true. But we are like the small lad who must be told and retold at every nightfall that going to sleep really isn't the end, that it's just a wonderful way to get ready for a new beginning.

Flight Ten-Four

That shudder we felt,
  Shivering the great ship end to end.
What was it, do you think?

Comes now the captain's voice:
  We are going down, he calmly says,
Two minutes to impact now.

Darling, take my hand, let me take yours.
  Together we have lived these years;
Let us be together now.

Thank God:
  No longer will we tarry,
Awaiting who will sicken first
  Or which must see the other go.

Never will we ever say goodbye.

Going Through the Valley

From about three thousand years ago, we have a literary gem considered by virtually all readers as precious and priceless. Over these many centuries, this ancient hymn of faith has been copied and recopied, published and republished, and, among other places, appears now as number twenty-three in the biblical book of Psalms.

After many readings over many years, I recently discovered that I had always missed a really brilliant facet of this delightful gem. A single very significant word among the approximately 118 had somehow eluded me, the word *through*.

In this psalm, the ancient singer is saying that in a dark, shadowed valley he will not be afraid, because God will be with him and comfort him there. Giving reassurance of this, he writes, "Though I walk through the valley of the shadow…"

Here is the word that I so long overlooked— "through," through the valley. The writer is not walking "in" the valley, but through it, not plodding and groping about in the dark, but striding forward, passing through.

So now when I come to one of life's shadowed places, I know that I don't have to stop there and make camp with my miseries. Some may morbidly like to do this and there feel sorry for themselves; but, I trust, not I.

Whatever the valley to which I come, whether the valley of the shadow of death or any other this side of that valley, it is for me merely a passing place. However deep, however dark, my life's onward journey will not be ended there. I will go on, and there will be a sunlit summit somewhere beyond the valley's end.

Therefore, the next time the valley shadows are upon me, I am resolved to remember that it is I who am the traveler, not *they*. I will go on and I will leave the shadows in their valley far below. For I am going to the mountain, and no shadow can survive the sunlight of that summit.

TOGETHER AT LAST
(FOR TWO WHO MARRY LATE IN LIFE)

God of love who made us so,
   Thank you.

God of love who made us so
   And sent us forth on divergent ways
To go and search and seek and hope to find,
   These journeys have been long.
For all that we have found,
   Thank you.

Now at length near journey's end,
   Divergent trails traversed and done,
They merge.

We are together, we two of yours;
   Here we join hands and climb your chancel stair,
A sanctuary where only we may ever come,
   Where only you are ever Lord.
We stand before you now—
   You who sent us forth in love
To go and search and seek and hope to find,
   In the love we think you meant us for,

Hearts co-joined, our spirits one,
   We come to seek your blessing now.
Affirm this that we have together found.
   With your blessing, send us forth once again,
Apart no more, but hand in hand,
   Until the journey takes us home.

It Was All a Good Deal

The life of my closest youth-time friend, John Miller, was taken from him fifty-seven years ago in a battle of the Second World War. Ten percent of my high school classmates were dead within four years of graduation. Over the years, others of my contemporaries have dropped away one by one.

During all this time, however, it has been my good fortune to go right on living. I have passed many delightful vistas the shorter life span of John Miller would not permit him ever to reach. I have enjoyed views from summits many of my classmates never saw.

Living is high privilege! Living is good, and I have now used up a lot of time doing it! I have had more time than many, more than most perhaps. As a matter of fact, I've grown old doing it. I have grown old—living.

Now I feel, sometimes, the disabilities and limitations that normally come with aging. So what? All of this is but a small price to pay for all that. Complain about growing old? Never! Aging is but the price we pay for living.

No good thing comes without a cost. If I want a prolonged chance at living, then I must not complain if, near life's end, the good years begin to take their toll. I will look back and be thankful, and whatever discomforts I now feel, I will say from my heart: It was all a good deal!

Walking in Our Own Shoes

Once, as I was leaving a position I had held for several years, someone commented, "Your shoes will be hard to fill." I replied, "I'm taking my shoes with me." It's always that way, isn't it? Going, we always take our shoes, and those who follow must bring their own.

Coming and going in whatever sequence, no person ever really replaces another. Each will add or subtract, and things will not be the same. You can replace the battery in your car with a second just like the first, but persons are not all alike; each is unique.

A second husband or a second wife can never replace the former, nor should he or she be expected to. For better or worse, or some of both, there will be change; life goes on. Business executive, teacher, pastor, janitor, or whoever, each will go in some direction from where another left off.

This means, of course, that everyone matters. No one coming into the world will leave it quite as it was; everyone makes a difference—and this includes you and me. Do you wonder if your life has mattered? Well, it has, and it does, and it will.

No, you cannot be a Plato or an Alexander the Great or a Beethoven or an Einstein, but you are you, and this is enough. You may not yet have triggered an avalanche, but you have at least dropped a pebble into the sea, and the ripples have probably been larger and gone farther than you will ever know.

You see, at whatever point and in whatever way we join the ongoing march of humanity, let us not undertake the impossible task of filling the shoes of anybody else, but strongly and confidently walk in our own.

A Prayer for Autumn-Time

The child was five, beautiful, vigorous—and blind. He had never seen a flying cloud, or a flower, or the face of his father or mother. Often, however, his mother had taken him walking about the lawn or garden, had told him of lovely growing things, and let him touch the leaves of plants and feel the bark of the great oak trees. Sometimes she had painted for him word pictures of gentle landscapes and a mountain that rose in sweeping curves against the sky.

Then came a couple of April days when the child was ill and unable to go outside at all. In his little robe and slippers, he climbed onto his mother's lap, snuggled against her, and said, "Please be my eyes for me and see beyond the window." His mother put her arm around her little one, turned toward the great green world of the outdoors, and tried to help her child see what she saw there.

We, the grown-ups of our kind, like that sightless child also sometimes need some help for seeing. Yes, we are normally blessed with eyes to look upon the wonders of the world about us, but we often fail to see the magnificence of it all and the magnificence and meaning of life itself. Seeing not far beyond our narrow windows, we often grope about in small, dark spaces.

Our view of things can be limited to what is immediate and obvious, and all the while beyond our small circles of vision are vast and wonderful vistas we so seldom see.

Many have been aware of this, among them Earl Marlatt, a teacher under whose teaching I and certain others of my generation once sat. This gentle man gave us a prayer-hymn about life—its springtime, growing time, and autumn time. The first stanza begins, "Spirit of life, in this new dawn…" Then, at the last it is "evening time" when "weary feet refuse to climb." Here the poet addresses the "Spirit of Love," asking for vision to see, beyond the dark, the dawn—beyond the dark, the dawn! Whatever, in the passing seasons of our life, we may have seen or missed seeing, this prayer is surely an appropriate one as the days grow shorter and autumn leaves are falling.

After the Storm

It was during the dark days of the Second World War, and for Joe Spangler today was the very darkest of them all. Five months ago, he and Martha had been notified that their only son was dead somewhere in the South Pacific. In frail health at the time, Martha's condition rapidly worsened, and four and half months later Martha was also gone.

Today, as he sat alone on the old-fashioned porch swing, looking out upon the Nebraska countryside, Joe felt another wave of the awful loneliness that so often overswept him these days. He thought of the tornado that less than a week before had laid down a swath of ruin across his community. He felt as though it or something similar had laid waste his own heart, devastating the world he had known and loved.

What to do now? How to deal with it all? Which way to turn? Where to go from here? Or was there anywhere to go, anything ahead? It seemed to Joe that life was all questions and no answers. Slowly, the stricken man arose wearily from the swing, crossed the porch, walked out to the road, and turned north.

A mile away, he came upon the mangled remains of what only a week ago had been a farm home. There crouched amid the rubble, a tool in his hand, Robert Watkins seemed to be striving with something.

Approaching, Joe said, "What are you doing, Bob?" Standing to greet his neighbor, Bob replied, "Well, Joe, it looks like I'll have to start over now, and I am searching among the ruins to salvage what I can." Then, after a brief pause and with the slightest suggestion of a smile, he added, "And you know, Joe, I'm actually finding more than I thought I would."

Later, walking homeward, Joe Spangler found himself considering the two tornadoes—the one that had struck Bob and the one that had struck him. He thought: I, too, must search among the ruins and salvage what I can.

As time went on, he did. Like Bob, Joe, in course of time, found more than he had supposed he could. Within himself, he found strengths he never knew were there. Among his friends and neighbors, he found support that helped to hold him up. From his God, through faith, he found a grace great enough to carry him through.

When I learned all this about Joe, I offered a little prayer for me: Lord, help me, whatever tornado comes, to look diligently amid the ruin and to salvage from it whatever I can. Then, help me to reassemble the broken fragments. Yes, the pattern will be different, but perhaps it can have a beauty of its own.

THE RELEASE OF A SHUT-IN

I spoke with my wife one day about the death of a man I knew. Not knowing him herself, she asked, "Who was he?" And I replied, "He was an elderly shut-in."

I explained that for nearly ten years this aged gentleman had been confined to an upstairs bedroom of his house, limited to his wheelchair and his bed, unable to rise without aid or to stand alone or move about, held prisoner by a circumstance of health, very truly shut in. That day, at his funeral service, we had celebrated the release of a prisoner.

Now, he wasn't shut in anymore; he was no longer a prisoner of infirmity and pain; he was now cut loose from his bondage. For nearly ten years, the doctors had tried to release him, but they had failed. Now in an instant, death had set him free.

Perhaps it is better said that the instance of death was the occasion of his liberation. I doubt if death deserves any credit here, for I don't think death meant to do for the old man the favor it did. Overestimating its power, it dared to lay a hand on him; and when it did, I think it must have drawn back with a start, surprised. For in that instant something snapped loose, and the old man was set free.

From that moment, he no longer struggled to lift an arthritic arm or open a swollen eye, for he didn't need these now. No longer did he need to strain against the prison walls of pain, for suddenly he had overleaped that high, gray parapet that for so long had been closing around him. He was loosed and set free; never again could anything ever shut him in.

OF STRINGS AND FEATHERS

The Americans who lived on our continent before the Europeans came were in general a deeply spiritual people. Among them, the physical world and the spiritual one were equally valid aspects of a single reality. Everybody lived in two worlds.

These two worlds, however, were not equally accessible or equally understood. Although the physical was obvious and easily touched, much effort and great discipline were normally required to be in touch with the other, and various means were used to make contact with it.

There was the common belief that dreams were such a means. During sleep, good dreams or bad ones could move in upon the human consciousness and profoundly affect all of life. The good kind of dream could provide the dreamer an inspiration or a guidance that he would live by ever afterward. Bad dreams could generate a sense of futility and a hopelessness from which the dreamer would never recover.

By night, dreams good and bad floated about in the atmosphere. They went about seeking minds to enter and dwell in, and the sleeper hoped that only the good ones would come.

Hence the "dream catcher." This was a small device made mostly of stings and feathers, usually eight strings and one feather. It was suspended in the air somewhere near the sleeper, there to catch the good dreams and screen out the bad ones. Because infant children had so much of life yet ahead of them, their dreams were especially important, and often miniature dream catchers were hung near their sleeping places.

I don't know if these dream-catching devices, for either child or adult, were at all effective—whether or not they provided any control of sleep-time dreaming. But I know this: There is known and experienced among us another kind of dreaming, a wide-awake kind, and we do have ways of exercising enormous amounts of control over this one.

The late Dr. Martin Luther King, Jr. once gave a magnificent and famous address in which a single phrase was repeated like the refrain of a song. That phrase was "I have a dream." By this, Dr. King was saying he had a hope, an aspiration, a goal, a destination to aim for.

This kind of wide-awake dreaming is within the reach of every living person. Such dreams are not snared from the air as they go floating by; they are generated in the human mind and spirit, and each person has the final say as to what will be generated there.

Nor are these dreams the fitful, flighty things that come by night and fade in the light of day; rather, they take hold and will not let go. They tend to put life into focus. As one of our poets has written, "He whom a dream hath possessed knoweth no more of roaming."

It is never too early and never too late to be so possessed. To be a dreamer comes most naturally for the very young and the very old, perhaps it is in their gift for dreaming that the two have the most in common. Let's make these wide-awake dreams bright and beautiful and good. We can, you know; we cannot catch them by use of stings and feathers, but we can create them from deep within ourselves.

THANKS FOR THE GIFT

A long-time friend was born the same year I was. I therefore have a good way of knowing how old she is. Recently, however, when we were together with a group of others, I overheard a conversation in which I learned from her that she is now nine years younger than I! This is a notable achievement if you can pull it off, and a very satisfying one if you want to be younger than you are!

But why should we want to be younger? Why should we want to give up a whole treasure chest of gifts that have been given to us? By gifts I mean all these years, all this time. We didn't create it, did we? Nor did we earn it. Like a gift from some anonymous benefactor, it has simply come to us.

What gift could ever be more precious, more useful, or of greater value than a gift of time? Just think what one can do with it; consider what certain others in the past have done with it.

Time is a gift we normally want more and more of. Birthdays are commemorated as occasions for compliment and congratulation—a kind of achievement. If we are seriously ill, we tend to worry that all our time may be about used up and that the illness can prevent our accumulation of anymore of it.

Strange, isn't it, that although year by year we want the gift to keep on coming in dependable annual increments, yet when many increments have accumulated and we consider the total, we tend sometimes to complain that we have too many of them!

I hope I'm appropriately thankful for all my accumulated years, and will always be. Many folks are never given nearly as many as I have already received, and I am enormously blessed by having been given them. I hope my sense of thankfulness is always so strong that it will never allow me to make out the gift as smaller and less valuable than it actually is.

INVISIBLE MEANS OF SUPPORT

We can read in the Bible of a time when Jesus of Nazareth walked on the water of a Palestinian lake. No, I don't know how he might have done that. I cannot do it, and I haven't known anyone else who could. I suspect, however that both you and I have seen some miracles altogether as amazing as that one.

Have you not sometime seen someone, smitten with trouble, who though stricken was not stuck down, but instead was buoyed up, and try as you would, you could not see what it was that held that person up? I have. Again and again, I have seen men and women and youth, bludgeoned by circumstance and yet upheld, sustained, with no visible means of support. Other persons have turned to one another in amazement and have said, "How can he do it?" or "How can she bear up under that?"

Around these persons nothing could be seen but the turbulence of storm. But there they stood, tall and straight and strong, as though on an invisible footing. Somehow they had leaned to walk on the water.

Because I have seen others do it, I know it can be done. So when comes the time, I hope I will have whatever it takes to do it also. For somewhere ahead of me, in the journey that will be mine, I'll probably come to some bleak and stormy time and will walk on slippery edges of gulfs that would swallow me up.

I am helped by something Moses once said concerning God. In his farewell address, this great Hebrew leader proclaimed to his people: "The eternal God is your dwelling place, and underneath are the everlasting arms." A means of support? Certainly.

KNOWING WHAT IS IN THE DARKNESS

The night was dark, and I was a very small boy. There was no moon, and heavy clouds shut out the light of every star. I was walking with my father along a narrow mountain path—a "cow path," as they say in the hills—a path wide enough for just one.

The terrain was strange to me, but my father had been there before, and he knew it well. He said, "Stay directly behind me, son, and stay close." Needless to say, I did!

My father knew what was in the darkness. I didn't know, but he knew, and I trusted him.

Many times since that night, as I have traveled life's ways; I have walked on other paths unknown and strange to me. Here too, sometimes, clouds have obscured the sky, and the darkness has been too dense for seeing.

No longer a timid and trembling lad with a trusted father to follow, but now, responsibility laden, I must find my way through some dark and dismal night. The usefulness of my sight depends on light, and there is none. I cannot see what is anywhere ahead; I know only that I must go there and meet whatever it is. I can imagine dangers on every hand, nameless perils that may await the very next step I take. I am tempted to draw back in fear, but I must go on.

No, I cannot see what is in the darkness, but I think I have learned a little about walking close to One who knows. Long ago a noble penman wrote this: "God knows what is in the darkness." I believe that; and if I walk close to God, and if I trust God, then I don't have to know.

EQUIPMENT FOR THE JOURNEY

The God who is "from everlasting to everlasting" is surely also the God who is from day to day. This is the way we need him—day by day. Come to think of it, this is the way we need everything.

In the beginning, life hands us the empty luggage and says, "Now you pack for the journey." We soon learn, however, that the journey is too long and the luggage too small; we discover that we'll have to replenish our supplies as we go.

Life is not a machine with a fuel tank that we can fill once and run to emptiness. It is rather a possibility-of-filling that we can take with us along the way.

Life is not like a motor-powered vessel, fully supplied with oil or coal, fueled for the whole voyage before it starts. Life has more in common with a wind-driven vessel, with sails daily set to catch whatever winds are stirring. It doesn't carry the winds with it but meets them where they are and catches them as it can.

Life is not so much like a gasoline- or diesel-powered coach as it is an electric trolley that must keep its antenna on the power wire. By maintaining this connection with the source of power, the energy for going forward is there when needed.

All of this, I think, is to say this very important thing: The equipment needed for life's journey is *capacity*. It is the ability and the willingness to receive help as help is needed, guidance as guidance is needed, whatever is needed when the need is there. It is the perpetual openness to receive, a continuous communication with the sources, and the confidence that there will be a way.

The night can be dark and the country strange, the roads unfamiliar and steep and rough in places. You start out by auto on an urgent drive that will take the night. You turn on the headlights, and by this light you can see a hundred yards ahead. That's all. There are hundreds of miles to go, and every mile is dark. You move your car forward, and as you move the light goes before you, not all at once an illumination of the whole length of the road, but at any one segment of it all the light you will need. Power and light are generated as you go.

Life is from day to day. So are the resources for seeing it through.

SOMETHING BEYOND

The dedicated artist, painting, runs at length into something his art cannot capture, so he must stand helpless in its presence. The devoted poet, writing, sooner or later encounters something her language cannot express; she is unable to say all she feels. The disciplined philosopher, thinking, runs into something beyond thought. The methodical scientist, searching, runs into mysteries yet unfathomed. May it be that one who ventures to the perimeters of his own being will find himself touching fingertips with God?

The learned astronomer, probing the heavens, considers the celestial orbs, all outward bound as though flung from one gigantic hand. Will they go on forever or come back together again? He or she doesn't know. How did it all begin, this vast existence? A "big bang" perhaps? If so, what triggered it? What determined when the beginning would be? Something necessarily, but what? If there was nothing before and then suddenly came this stupendous explosion, what was it that exploded? Something necessarily, but what? The astronomer doesn't know.

At this point the astronomer encounters an essential unknown. Some powerful factor is necessarily involved here, but what? So the astronomer and his or her fellow scientists have given a name to this essential unknown: they call it a "singularity." This means, I suppose, something unique, one-of-a-kind, a nonconformist entity transcending normal patterns. But one thing is sure about it: It simply has to be; for without this essential unknown all theories of existence fall into disarray.

Perhaps we should spell the word *singularity* with a capital "S." Why? Because what for some may be an essential unknown may to others of us be known as God.

Good people in various scientific disciplines have long pondered the puzzles of existence, asking why things are as they are and behave as they do. It is generally agreed that somewhere there must be something that explains it all. This has compelled the scientific world to embark on an urgent quest. This is the search for what is commonly called "the unifying principle." Such a principle is required, it is said, to explain and make sense of everything. These seekers are convinced there is such a principle, there just has to be. But thus far they have not found it. It is anticipated that this discovery, if and when made, will be the most important scientific news of all time.

Perhaps we should also spell the words *unifying principle* with capital letters. Why? Because some persons of faith may have discovered that principle already, and there may be a clue for us in a couple of biblical passages concerning the Divine One. It is written here that "he sustains all things by his powerful word" and that "in him all things hold together."

Whether artist, poet, philosopher, or scientist, whoever the seekers are and whatever they are searching for, when we have gone as far as mind and spirit can reach, we confront an ultimate truth: There is something beyond. Dealing with a "singularity" we do not understand or a "principle" we have not yet found, we may be nearer than we know to an encounter with God. You and I, when we feel our spirits upward drawn, know deeply: There is something, Someone, beyond.

Part V

Detours Always Go Somewhere

Ahead of you on the highway are flashing lights, a barricade, an arrow pointing to the right or left, and a one-word message: *Detour.*

"Oh no!" you say. But you go the way the arrow points: you leave the main highway; you turn into the narrow road; and you slow down. You've never traveled this way before, and you are uncertain what lies ahead. Will it be long? Will it be rough? You are concerned about the delay.

But you know, really, that this is not a dead-end road. It is a detour, and this means that it will come out somewhere. You know this road is simply another way to where you are going. You don't know why the main road is closed to you, and you wish it weren't; but there must be a reason. The detour isn't your first choice of ways, but all things considered, it must be the best. The detour route may not be the easiest and most direct; but under the circumstances, it must be the most correct.

In life, aren't we often confronted with detour signs? We are going along well; the road is open; the goal is ahead; the milestones of achievement go rhythmically flashing by. Then suddenly, unexpectedly perhaps, it's "Detour!" It's an illness, a trouble, a difficulty of some kind, an interruption. The highway ahead is closed, and we must turn aside to travel by another road. It's unfamiliar, strange; we wonder how long it will be and where it will come out. We are inclined to fret and resist and complain.

In our living, however, we need to learn a lesson we have learned from our driving: A detour is not the result of some malicious conspiracy to force us off the highway. When the easier road must be closed for awhile, this road is provided as an alternate way. It will link up at length; you can count on that. It isn't the usual thoroughfare, but it will get you there just the same.

THREE ROOMS THAT MAKE A HOME

If you were selecting the three rooms of greatest importance in the making
of a home, which three would you choose? Rooms for cooking, eating,
sleeping? These are necessary and quite practical, yes. But such rooms make
only a house. The names I would place in nomination are these:

First, *The Living Room*. Think of it as more than a certain physical space
comprised of a numbered amount of square footage. Think of it as being
wherever living takes place in a house, wherever people share, wherever the
inhabitants enter into experience together. We may go out to shop or earn
or learn and for some kinds of recreational activity, but, mostly, we come
home to live. The notion that the essential requirements of life are satisfied
by "going out" is as patently false as the notion that everything really enjoy-
able is to be found somewhere outside the home. The truth is that people
who really live do most of their real living at home.

Second, *The Parlor*. It is the same room as the living room, you may say.
Perhaps. But it accents an important aspect of family living. The word
parlor is from the French *parlez*, meaning "to talk." The parlor is a conversation place, or, of more importance perhaps, a conversation opportunity.
It is where mind meets mind, where thought touches thought. It is where
encounter happens and, happening, can implant ideals, generate courage,
lift vision, widen horizons. The character of the conversation in the home
is of critical importance. Here we have the finest of all opportunities for
personal growth and enrichment.

Third, *The Drawing Room*. Originally, this room was the "withdraw-
ing" room, its place and space the same as the others just mentioned. It is
that place into which one can withdraw to find renewal and recovery, the
place where a man, woman, or child—weary, troubled, misunderstood by
the world outside—can find refuge in the shelter of others who care. Here
is rest from labor and recovery from hurt. Here, bruised by venture into the
world outside, one comes home into the sheltering companionship of
family love and finds strength to carry on and to venture forth again. Here
is a soothing hand on a fevered brow, a handclasp, an embrace, a kiss on a
tear-stained cheek—and power for anything! Here, in the face of battering
difficulties, is the irrepressible worth of the miracle words "I love you."

To Be Bewildered Is Not to Be Lost

Daniel Boone, the American explorer and scout, survived his wilderness exploits and lived to the age of eighty-six. Late in his life, someone asked if he had ever been lost in the woods. With a twinkle, the indomitable old man replied, "No, never lost—but I was bewildered once for three days." Not lost, merely bewildered!

A man of less courage and perceptivity would probably have panicked in much less than three days; and had he panicked, he probably would have been lost. There's a difference between bewilderment and lostness. Even a Daniel Boone may sometimes be bewildered but almost never lost.

A person in a state of bewilderment is only bewildered unless he gives himself up for lost, and then he is. A state of bewilderment may be thrust upon us from without by the conditions around us, but lostness is a condition that arises within us, a response we make to circumstance.

You can lose your way for a while without being lost, even as you can sometimes fail without being a failure. Only that person who has given in to failure is a failure, and the only traveler who is lost is the one who has given up all hope of finding his way. You are not lost simply because you don't know where you are.

To travel in a trackless land, not knowing what is next, is not to be lost. To lose view of the last known landmark, to go beyond the edge of the map, is not to be lost. To go where no one has gone before is not to be lost. Only he is lost who, wherever he is, gives up in despair, sits down in hopelessness, and never ventures again to try.

Two Worlds Within Us

Values are best seen in contrast. The warmth of a winter fire is most appreciated if we have some knowledge of the cold it keeps away. Have you noticed: One is most thankful for a smooth highway after many miles on a rough one.

If you would thrill to the beauty of a rainbow, see first the dark, wind-driven storm out of which it came. If you would picture the power of a great ocean ship, see it not in the harbor, but against the backdrop of a storm-torn sea. If you would enjoy the full loveliness of a rose, see it against the rugged rocks and barren cliffs and among the thorns where it grows. If you would really appreciate the springtime sun, feel first the sting of winter's cold blast.

It is when considered alongside its alternative that anything of value stands forth in the full dimension of its worth. We live in two worlds, and the one helps us to a greater appreciation of the other. In whatever direction we turn, the happy and the sad, the pretty and the ugly, the good and the bad are usually only a few paces or a few minutes away.

Two worlds touch each other in our souls also. They seem to come in from somewhere and meet at the very center of our being: pain and pleasure, sorrow and joy, travail and triumph. How frequently it happens that the joys are greater because sorrows have first come and have stretched out big places for joy to abide in. Somehow, the soul exercised by a sorrow seems more competent to accommodate a joy. How often, too, smiles are more genuine because tears have come before.

No doubt, one can enjoy a mountaintop most if he has walked sometime in some deep, dark valley.

You see, trying as they can be, our traumas aren't altogether harmful to us. They are painful, yes, but painful like the pain from a surgeon's knife excising a place for health. The sorrow and grief that from time to time invade our spirits really intend us no harm. They can, in fact, help us if we let them. For joys will also come, and these, like the rose seen against the barren backdrop, will be most fully felt in contrast.

It's Great to Be Trusted

Our farm home was near a creek where the road crossed without benefit of bridge. After heavy rains, when the water was high, automobiles frequently stalled in midstream, their engines "drowned."

Then would come a call for help. My father would harness our team of horses, Dick and Pet. Taking a heavy chain, he would go down to the creek, hitch to the stalled car, and pull it out of the water. After some drying of spark plugs and wires, the motorist could usually get it going again.

On one such occasion, the driver discovered that the crankcase of his new Chevy had somehow been flooded with water. This meant that it must be drained and refilled with fresh, clean oil. The nearest oil was two miles away at the village of Greenville. I was eight or nine then and had never gone to town alone, but my dad said that I might go and fetch the oil.

He then stripped the harness from old Pet and set me atop her bare back. The motorist put two one-dollar bills in my hand. I dug my heels into the flanks of our family's most beloved animal, and we took off!

No patriot running an enemy blockade ever experienced higher exhilaration or felt more heroic than I did that day. I don't think anyone or anything could have diverted me or stopped me. *I was being trusted!* I was believed in! It was as though a fire had been lit within me. I felt big and strong and brave.

Isn't it always so? It should be. If we possess the stuff of real humanity, to be trusted is to be inspired. Responding to the trust of others, we experience something that rises warm and strong and brave within us. Failing this, our souls must be dead or nearly so, for to be trusted comes as a wake-up call to stir whatever spark of life is there. If being trusted, either by those of earth or heaven, cannot move us to loyalty and heroism, then, pray tell, what can?

A Midday Meditation

I stood at the mountain's summit
   When the dawn was in the sky,
And I saw the crimson wonder
   Of the world before me lie.

A bold new strength was in me
   In the marvel of that hour.
It welled and swelled and swept me
   With surging tides of power.

I stood transfixed by all I saw
   And by all I felt within,
And deeply vowed to hold forever
   The dream that held me then.

I seized the brush that was offered me
   And faced my canvas there,
Resolved my art would stand supreme
   Above all masters everywhere.

Timorous moments I stood there waiting,
   Moments of unwaiting time.
Timid of heart, I stood there pondering,
   And the sun began to climb.

And while I pondered, waiting there,
  The brush still in my hand,
There came a change upon the sky
  And all across the land.

And, my canvas still untouched,
  The crimson turned to gray;
The eastern glory slowly faded,
  The rose-tints died away.

Mute, I stood and watched the sun
  Climb upward to the noon,
In my heart a sadness and a longing
  For the dawn that died so soon.

And now, in early afternoon,
  A questing soul that will not rest,
My morning gone, my task undone,
  I turn to face the west.

The dream is gone but is not dead,
  And, I think, can never die:
It haunts me still as though awaiting
  Another crimson sky.

For the sunset has a glory too,
  Not unlike the dawn;
And this perchance my soul will feel,
  As it felt the glory gone.

Perhaps in the crimson twilight,
  When the rose-tints reappear,
The dream may fire and stir again
  In one last glory here—

May flash and flame and burn again
  As in that dawn of long ago,
May flash and flame and die there then
  In that bright afterglow.

The Courage to Become

The story is told of a small boy who, when asked "Who made you?" answered, "I ain't done yet!" Had he been asked "Who are you?" he might well have replied, "I don't know yet." Correct answers in both cases, I think.

None of us know who we are at first, and it usually takes a good many years to find out. As a distinguished-appearing gentleman strolls through the office, someone asks, "Who's that?" and another answers, "That's the president of our company, a very competent fellow." Back home, where he grew up, folks say, "I didn't know he had that in him." It took a while to find out; neither they nor he knew at first.

And, sadly, some people never really discover what is in them, never really find out who they are. "He hasn't found himself yet"; how often this is said of some floundering fellow, and the expression well put.

Some of us get sidetracked on the road to self-discovery and never really arrive; we get stranded along the way. Each of us is unique; and it can be said that we will never find out who we are if we always go along with whatever crowd we happen to be in. The route to self-realization calls for more careful steering.

With the demands for conformity that come at us from all sides and the desire for comfort that is always present within us, we can easily get lost along the way. Most of us want to be "in" with an "in" crowd, or with some crowd that thinks it is in. Even the extreme nonconformist will get his kicks from being "in" with an "out" crowd.

In ideals and morals, we are inclined to go with the flow. The fear of being left out is deeply ingrained. We seek the comfort of class. Like the chameleon, we assume the color of wherever we are. It isn't easy, for instance, to say no to the yes crowd. Temptations are strong to fall in with the "anything goes" parade.

In this way we get lost, sidetracked, stranded. Pulled off course by the undercurrents, our ship never arrives. Life never reaches full magnitude. Thus, having spent all our years, we end up not knowing who we really were.

It takes courage to become ourselves. It's easy to get squeezed into someone else's mold. It's sometimes hard to hold a course firmly when other ships are zigzagging all over the sea, or to steer by a distant star when the sirens are singing from an island nearby.

In all our years, intermittently and constantly, we are in process of becoming. Life is so constituted that we will never fully become until we have followed the highest ways that were open to us for as long and as far as we possibly can. It will be only when we have finished this pilgrimage that we will find out who we really were and are.

The Soul's Supreme Adventure

To speak about love is to risk being misunderstood. This wonderful word has of late suffered horrible indignities. It has been in some circles so grossly perverted as to become a caricature of its real self—in the language of poet Edwin Markham, "plundered, profaned, and disinherited."

But we cannot give it up or, I think, surrender it to its abusers; we have no other English word to put in its place. So I want to speak about love—love in its true and traditional character. What I want to say is this: Loving is the soul's supreme adventure.

Most of us are fascinated by adventure. We are thrilled by adventure stories: Sir Galahad going for the grail; Marco Polo going; Christopher Columbus going; Neil Armstrong going. When we really love, something of us is going, moving out, venturing forth on a mission of doing, serving, lifting, helping.

Loving isn't academic; it is actual. It isn't static; it is dynamic. Something *happens* when we love; there is transaction. From within its sheltered place, love opens a door and steps outside, tentatively moving perhaps on timid feet, but moving nonetheless—reaching, going. What will befall it out there? What joy or pain? Will the air be warm or chill? Whatever awaits, love goes, for it's the nature of love to do so.

Someone says, "I won't put myself out." Well, when we love, we do. We venture beyond our zone of safety, beyond our secure boundaries. We move out to where we are vulnerable, and there's risk and adventure in that. You see, when we love, when we truly love, we are investing something of what we are in somebody or something outside ourselves.

It was Jesus who said that the first two commandments are these: Love God and love our neighbor. If we think there's no adventure in that, then we've never lived it. To give ourselves lovingly and obediently to God, going where God calls, doing what God wishes, this is adventure; we never know where that road will lead. To enter into the sufferings of a neighbor, or to offer loving response to one who has wronged us, or to feel the anguish of a Mary Magdalene who falls soul-sick at our feet—here our venturing love is leading us into regions beyond.

But it is for adventure the soul is made. Love is the motive power that can set it free and send it soaring. Refugees perhaps from the disagreeable or the uncomfortable, we often take refuge within ourselves; we turn inward and close the door against all that is out there. So we become prisoners in shelters of our own design. With most of us, love alone has power to open our prison gates and lead us forth on ventures wide and wonderful.

The Years Are My Friends

I have resolved to be always on friendly terms with the friendly years. I will meet them, greet them, and welcome them as I would all good friends: as they come, as they go; sometimes rushing, racing, sometimes slowly passing—but always coming, always going.

They are made of something called time, and time is on the side of right and beauty and truth. Justice may be thwarted momentarily, but it can wait for the years, and it can depend upon them for vindication and honor. Truth can await the confirmation of the centuries, and it will have it. More arguments are settled by the passing years than by anything else, and eventually the years will settle them all.

Why, then, should I not look upon the years as my friends? Already I have met and known quite a number. Some have been hard, but all have been good. These I have known, and others I will yet meet; I believe that all of them mean well for me, and I trust them. Eventually, they will answer all my unanswered questions and solve all the problems that plague and vex me now.

You see, the ongoing years do not go by to tease and taunt us as they pass; they are going somewhere, and they invite us to go with them. They intend to come out in a beautiful place, and they'd like to have us with them when they arrive. We do them wrong to complain that they make us older or to fight with them along the way. If we choose an adversarial relationship with the passing years, we deny ourselves the congenial traveling companionship we might have had.

Oh yes, the years are our friends, better friends than we know, perhaps; they help us in ways we've thought but little about. They come to carry us forward to higher and better things, to conduct us through Elysian lands and bring us at last to sunlit summits we but dimly see from here.

WISHES, WANTS, AND DREAMS

Considering what may yet happen to us, we usually have our preferences, don't we? We like things to work out for us in agreeable ways, and we would normally welcome any assurance that it might be so. A good fairy could make us very happy should she appear and say, "According to your *wishes* be it done for you."

Assuming the fairy could make good on her promise, think what this would mean: all our wishes would be fulfilled, all we wish for would be ours.

Or suppose the fairy says, "According to your *wants* be it done for you." Whatever we would like we would have; whatever we want to happen would happen as we want it to.

Or suppose the fairy says, "According to your *dreams* be it done for you." Then out of our fanciful world would suddenly emerge the real, with every street and spire precisely as we had dreamed it to be.

Thus, wishes, wants, and dreams all fulfilled and realized, how very satisfied we should be.

But suppose the good fairy makes yet another offer, one very similar in most respects. Suppose she says, "According to your *faith* be it done for you." What then? Would we really want it this way?

Yes, we may answer—without thinking. But do think about it: Is our faith so great? Suppose it were indeed done for us in proportion to the dimensions of our faith; suppose only that which our faith calls for ever came—only this and nothing more? Where would this leave us? What would our condition be then?

Wishes, wants, and dreams unlimited! But faith can be so small! Should that good fairy come to me with her generous offer, I suspect that my instant response would be: Oh, how I wish now that my faith had been larger!

You see, wanting something to happen and believing it will are two very different exercises of mind and spirit. We can want something to happen and be afraid it won't.

For instance, what about tomorrow? What do we expect of it? What do we really believe about it? Let's be thankful that our tomorrows have many times turned out better than we feared they would. The future frequently delivers more to us than our apprehensions have allowed us to expect.

Most of my life, I have received more than I have believed for. Therefore, when I am tempted now to complain that I have believed for some things that never came, I hope I can remember the many that have, and beyond that, all those uncalled for in my faith and sometimes transcending all my dreams. Remembering this, I will trust Providence, in the future as in the past, to give more than my small faith has called for.

Perspective on Pain

I hurl my questions against the dark,
   Nor pause to listen for reply;
I shout protest against all that hurts,
   Forever asking why.
As though suffering were something new
   And I had just discovered pain,
I send my screams into the night
   And bitterly complain.

But agony is as old as human feeling—
   And perhaps it was before.
It walks the world with measured tread
   And knocks at length on every door.
So what cause have I, of humankind,
   To whimper and chafe and whine,
When, in all its pillaging door to door,
   It comes one day to mine?

Don't Touch That Stone!

There it is, the stone that I might take up and hurl at somebody. It is within easy reach, readily available to me, and is such as to make an effective missile. It is the unkind or hateful word that I can speak, the insinuating remark that I can make, the critical or cynical thing that I might say. I should never touch it!

Such stones, maliciously or wantonly cast, can in moments destroy life structures that were decades in the building. These stones, lethal weapons really, are available in a variety of forms: lies, half-truths, double-talk, innuendoes, suggestions, leading questions, and even truth of such character that it is better left untold.

So here is that stone that I can reach out and pick up, and there is someone to throw it at; there always is. Targets abound. By rules of the stone-throwing mentality, anybody is fair game. Actually, of course, there is no person so nearly perfect but that some fault can somewhere be found. But why pick at it? Will my victim be helped if I do? Will I?

Who am I to cast this stone anyway? Am I so much better than the one at whom I aim it? I may think so; and I may, by this act, seek to boost an illusion of my own superiority; but I ought to know that I do not ever really elevate myself by putting another down.

A group of strongly opinionated men once brought a woman to Jesus of Nazareth, demanding to know if Jesus thought she should be stoned to death. In response, Jesus offered a striking proposal: "Let the man who is without sin among you be the first to cast a stone at her." One by one, the men dropped their stones and sneaked away.

Should he propose the same to me, I suspect I would want to sneak away with the others. So I think I'll drop whatever stones I've been carrying around and leave them where they fall.

It's in Relationship That We Live

You are conscious of yourself, aware of *being*. You can say "I *am*" and have some sense of what it means to *be*. How, though, do you *identify* yourself? I ask, "Who are you?" and you reply, "I am John W. Doe." But you haven't answered my question; you haven't told me who you are. You have, instead, told me about something that is *yours*, your name. Now I know what your name is, but I still don't know who you are. Actually, you have said, "My name is John W. Doe." That name *belongs* to you, but who *are* you?

You may now take your Social Security card from your wallet, look at it, and say, probably with a smile, "I am number. . ." Again, you have told me about something that is yours. Is there no way you can identify yourself?

You think of the lady who sat across the table from you at breakfast this morning, and you say, "I am the husband of Jane Doe." Good! Now you are telling me something of who you *are*. You are a husband. Immediately your mind turns to your children, and you say, "I am a father."

Now, getting into the spirit of the thing, you look up and see your country's flag flying, and you say, "I am a citizen of the United States." Your eye catches a gleam of sunlight on the spire of a nearby church, and you say, "I am a Christian." You look up at tufted clouds floating against the blue, and thoughtfully you say, "And, yes, I suppose I am a child of God."

You come to realize, then, that you *have* a name and number, but that you *are* husband, father, citizen, church member, and child of God. That is, you are someone in relationship with a wife, a child, a country, a church, and God. It is, you see, actually in relationship that you live.

So it is with all of us. All these relationships of ours—how very important they are, how significant, how precious, how rewarding, how fulfilling!

If, over the years, we are careful to build a strong structure of satisfying and congenial relationships, then, at length, we have all around us this zone of comfort in which we can find peace and can dwell securely.

In preparation for life's concluding years, we are, of course, well advised to attend to our physical well being and financial security, to anticipate the changes the years will bring. But we can make no preparation that will be more meaningful to us than to develop on all sides relationships that are congenial and fulfilling.

Gradually, with passing time, certain facets of our life will diminish or disappear, but good solid relationships will be ours to the end. Among family, friends, associates, with other persons everywhere, and with God, bound by strong cords of appreciation, devotion, and love, our relationships will be there to comfort and sustain us, to move us and inspire us, even when little else may remain.

Conquering the Grasshopper Complex

It was a good and desirable land—so reported all twelve of the spies Moses had sent into Canaan. It was rich, productive, and abundant, and Moses and his pilgrim people were convinced they had rightful claim to it. But the land was occupied. Would they be able to take it?

Ten of the twelve said no. Although it was a bountiful land, there were fortified cities "walled up to heaven" and giants, "the sons of Anak." These ten said, "We were in our sight as grasshoppers, and so we were in theirs."

Two of the twelve, however, had a different opinion. Yes, they said, there are indeed walled cities and giants, but so what? We are strong and the Lord is with us. They said, "Let us go up and occupy the land, for we are well able to overcome it."

Here were two views of the same circumstance. One saw conquest as impossible; the other saw it as easily achievable. Both understood the difficulties; the difference lay in the way they understood themselves. One said: alongside this task, we are of grasshopper size. The other said: Yes, the difficulties are great, but we are greater.

We have here what I choose to call the grasshopper complex, whose victims are those who see themselves defeated before they start. They won't tackle a task unless they are sure they are much bigger than it is; they will risk nothing; they want everything to come with a guarantee. They must be certain of victory before they will begin the struggle, sure of winning before they will attempt the race. They will match themselves only against the most trifling tasks, the most mediocre undertakings.

Too bad. Any land worth conquering will have some giants in it. There are giants in the land of education, in the land of marriage, in the land of labor, in the land of parenting, in the land of character development, in the land of aging. There are giants in all good lands, obstacles to be overcome.

Only wastelands can be occupied without effort; no good land can be possessed except by some degree of struggle. Oh yes, we must recognize the power of the giants who may be there, but never overlook the fact that when we stand to fight them, mightier giants can arise within us.

The offspring of Anak, wherever found, will never have the last word; courage will. In trying to conquer anything, the fear of what can happen to us personally must be overcome by the confidence that what we fear won't happen and by the courage that says that if what we fear does happen, it won't matter all that much.

At the Edge of Our Map

Have you sometime seen those ancient maps of the world, the kind that were made when much of Earth was still unknown and when most people believed it flat? Beyond the known areas, primitive mapmakers pictured what imagination saw as being there. Along the edge there may have appeared a bottomless abyss where sailors might plunge into oblivion, or on the seas monstrous serpents waiting to swallow whole ships. After all, the unknown was supposed to be terrifying, was it not?

Among the ancients, however, there were some who saw it otherwise. Hence came Christopher Columbus, defying the serpents and doggedly believing the East could be reached by sailing west.

For many among us now, as for many long ago, the unknown is still terrifying. But faith sees it otherwise and will bravely lift all anchors and unfurl all sails to whatever winds may come.

We now know a lot more about geography than was known in ancient times, but no more is known about time itself. Whatever the time, we always stand at the edge of our map.

Whatever number of days we may have logged, tomorrow remains a mystery; we do not know what it holds for us. We may sometimes think we know; we may have a fairly good idea about it; but we can never know for sure. In most respects, we know no more about our tomorrows than the ancients knew about theirs. We live in a continual encounter with the unknown. Should we be terrified by it? Not if we are people of faith.

Faith is undismayed by the existence of mystery; she stands in her greatest glory when she stands in the presence of the unknown. We can therefore most rewardingly say "I believe" when we are most compelled to say "I don't know."

THINK AND BE THANKFUL

Suppose you are the only person left in the world. Suppose some calamity has overtaken the whole population of the earth and only you remain. Suppose you know that you are alone.

Great machines and great structures are everywhere around you. In the countryside, fields of growing grain lie verdant beneath the sun, and in green pastures cattle are grazing. All the gold in the banks is still there; all the jewels of the rich lie where they were left.

Now everything is yours. All you need do is reach forth your hand and take it; none will restrain you. But how will you use it? What will you do with it? What will it mean to you? What value will it have?

You stand in the midst of it all, and you are lonely. You may run the gold through your fingers until they burn; you may view the sparkle of diamonds until you are blind; but in the absence of other persons, what does it all mean?

Flowers still bloom; the sun still rises and sets in all the glory of eastern and western sky. Trees still bear their leaves and stars twinkle. As you survey all this, you weep in solitary grief, and there is no one to comfort you or to weep with you. You have discovered that all the things in the world are of no value if *things* are all you have. You have discovered that all value is ultimately *personal*.

But you are not the only person left in the world. Look about you. Do it now. And think. Think of the persons you have seen today and those you will see this week. Think of the voices you will hear, the eyes into which you will look, the hands you will touch. Think of the hearts that beat not far from your own, and of strangers, even, whose hearts are just as feeling and just as hungry as yours. Look, and think, and be thankful.

OUR THREE INFINITIVES

We live by three infinitives: to *be*, to *have*, and to *do*. It's essential to the best kind of good life to maintain an appropriate balance among these.

In one of the parables of Jesus of Nazareth there *was* a man who *had* five talents, and he *did* something with them; he lived well. There *was* a man who *had* three talents, and he *did* something with them; he lived well. There *was* a man who *had* one talent, and he *did nothing* with it; Jesus described him as cowardly, lazy, wicked, and unprofitable.

That man had infinitive trouble. He was afraid of the third infinitive; he was afraid to act. Spurning one of the three infinitives, he tried to live by two. All three are great and good to live by. Consider them:

It's great just to *be.* You *are.* You can say, "I *am.*" You are a *BEing,* a human BEing. If preliminary sequences had been somewhere a bit different, you *may never have been.* But you *are.* It's rather wonderful, isn't it?

It's wonderful also to *have.* To *have* the power to lift a hand at will. To *have* the power to move things about, to control action; it's an awesome and dangerous power. To *have* the ability to take the hand of another person in a clasp of fellowship, or in helpfulness, or in love. To *have* a voice for speaking, to convey meanings, express feelings, to make an impact, to *have* the skill to sew a seam or dive a nail, to change the structure of things. To *have* the ability to create—to paint a picture or write a poem—to add somewhat to the total wealth of the world's experience. To *have* the capability of reason, to put two thoughts together, to deduce the meanings of things, to probe mysteries, to search for understanding.

It's wonderful also to *do,* to express being through doing, to act out what is built in, actually to lift the hand you can lift, to speak the word you can speak; for it is in doing that being is fulfilled, and it is in using well what we have that having is justified.

SEEING IN FULL CIRCLE

"Circumstance" is that which stands around: "stance" (stand) and "circum" (around). When we speak of our circumstances, we are speaking of what stands around us and bears in upon us in some way and is therefore affecting us by its presence within the scope of our current experience.

Sometimes we complain about our circumstances, feeling that they encumber or restrain us. Especially as we grow older, this is a temptation we must strive with all our might to resist. At any age we may feel restricted or limited by our circumstances, fenced in, imprisoned. We can feel that our circumstances will not permit us to do what we ought to or want to. We can excuse ourselves from this or that good deed or endeavor because of what we see as our circumstances. For the same reason, we sometimes deny ourselves certain privileges or pleasures. The pitiful consequence is that, because of what we view as our circumstance, we often give up on living, or at least on a considerable portion of it.

We often have this problem with circumstances: the problem is that we are inclined to view them selectively, seeing some but not all. To get a full view of circumstance, all that stands around, we need to make a complete 360-degree turn; we need to look all the way around, never blinking.

Much of the time, we fail to see in full circle. We get our vision fixed on some adverse sort of circumstance on one side and never turn to see the favorable circumstance that may be on the other.

For instance, there is the fellow who complains about his poverty but scarcely takes note of his good health. Or there is the one who wails about a ten-percent increase in the cost of living but neglects to note that his income has increased twice as much.

Each of us is a part of a big picture, and we need to see ourselves there, else we may become mired down in some dreary corner of it.

Further, we ought to understand that there is something more enduring about life than can ever be experienced in any of its incidentals. We are on our way somewhere, and the whole journey is immeasurably larger than any one mile of the road.

We live in a fantastic environment of circumstance, so let us not give exclusive attention to the bramble at our feet or the thorn that pricks us in the side. When we lift our eyes to the wide horizons, we know that among our circumstances is the light of a million brightly shining stars. What a pity if we never see them!

On Being a Follower

In our time, a lot is said about leadership. The qualities that make for leadership are much discussed. Schools and other institutions emphasize the development of leaders, and this is commendable.

May I suggest, however, that in our world there is always a lot more following than there is leading. It seems to me it's time someone says something about the art of being a good follower. Following can be a rewarding way of life, or it can be a disaster. Much could be said about following, and probably should be said. I offer here five observations concerning the art of followship:

1. Choose whom or what to follow. The choice is yours, you know. Remember that anybody or anything can get a following, and usually does. Any person, any idea, any way of thinking can start a parade, and there are

those who will fall in like rats behind the Pied Piper. Therefore, don't choose your leader solely because of the direction in which the crowds are moving. Ask: "Where am I being taken and why?" Many say, "Follow me," offering their various persuasions. Consider them well—and with caution.

2. Your choice made, get up and get going. Commit yourself to a discipleship. You will never know how reliable your leader is unless you stay up close and observe with care. Look to your leader, but don't lose your mind, for a good follower needs to be in command of a good mind. Any leader worthy of a following will want and welcome the full-functioning vigor of the minds of all who follow him or her. Reject any who will not let you think.

3. Be faithful to your commitment, but don't surrender your conscience. Don't close your eyes and go stumbling blindly along. Do remember that any leader who demands a blind following is unworthy of any following at all.

4. Reserve the right to deviate or to bail out. Leadership is a position of power, and there are some who don't handle power responsibly. Among these are many who covet positions at the head of some parade or other. Try to anticipate where your leader is going. If he or she turns into a blind alley or goes over a precipice, don't follow. Retain your powers of discretion.

5. If your leader is noble, follow nobly; but be prepared for some risk and sacrifice. If your leader is climbing a mountain, there will be some perilous places to pass. If your leader is pointing to a star, you will have to forgo the views of some other things along the way.

And do remember this: We of humankind, being who we are, no leader among us is worthy of a following who *isn't* climbing a mountain or pointing to a star.

Part VI

Getting Dividends from Detours

Years ago, as a relative and I were driving though the Susquehanna River country of northern Maryland, we came upon a section of highway that was closed for reconstruction. Much to our displeasure, we were forced to take a detour.

I have never forgotten that road, the route unchosen. It took us through some of the most beautiful rural settings I had ever seen. I was thrilled, excited, inspired by the beauty. But within an hour or so we were out of that area and headed into Washington.

A couple of decades later, I resolved to drive again among these pastoral scenes. I was unable, however, to find anything even remotely similar to the road I had traveled before. There was no difficulty in locating the main highway; but it hadn't been the main highway that had led me to the beauty I wished to see again. I needed first to locate the road I had enjoyed a number of years before, but I never found it.

Often I have thought: Had my relative and I had our first choice of roads that day, I never would have enjoyed the beauty of the countryside I saw. It had been only because we were forced onto a detour that I had seen it.

Thinking of this, I have thought of our life. Sometimes it's only when we are compelled to take some road of second choice that we experience the best of the journey. If we can get beyond our worrying about the detour and look around a little, we may see vistas of beauty we never dreamed were there and, passing on, may never see again.

Rich dividends often await us on life's detour roads. The perspectives are different there. Insights that might never come otherwise may sometimes be clearly read on the white ceilings of hospital rooms. A calamity may bring us to new appreciation of day-to-day blessings we have long taken for granted. The near loss of a loved one may inspire a profounder thankfulness for all we care about.

We normally give the more careful attention to the unfamiliar road. We are likely, therefore, to see more of it and to learn more from it. So, whenever in my journey across the years I come again upon that most unwelcome of road signs, I'll take the detour regretfully of course, but I'll try to see it through with eyes wide open for the good and beautiful that may appear along the way.

The Wonder of Being Human

Having been caught in a stupidity, one explains, "Well, you know I'm only human!"

Only human? Michelangelo was human, as were Shakespeare, Joan of Arc, Einstein, Mahomet, Plato, and the apostle Paul. It seems to me that being human is high class. Being human is to be associated with some rather exalted company.

Consider the quality of the company we humans keep. In all the world there isn't a scrap of great literature or a square inch of great art that was not brought into being by a human. There isn't anywhere a note of great music that did not well up from the depths of a human spirit. There has never been a great thought except it took shape in a human mind. Every hero or heroine you have ever heard of or read about was equally as human as you and I are.

Yes, of course, humans sometimes do dastardly things. We read about some of these people in the morning paper and hear about them on the evening news. Why do we hear about them? Because they are the exceptions. In some way and to some degree, they have betrayed their humanity. They have behaved uncharacteristically. They are not typical of our Kind. They are anomalous, and therefore they are news.

Never should we humans think of ourselves as condemned to membership in a substratum of existence. Actually, to be human is to occupy the highest place there is under heaven. We have no need to apologize for that. Nor have we any right to excuse our misbehaviors on the ground that we are human. That's a copout.

Our Changing Values

It's interesting, isn't it, the way our estimate of values changes with circumstance? What is cherished as a priority in one circumstance may have no appeal in another. Thus, yesterday's trinket can become tomorrow's treasure. Likewise, what was of great importance to us yesterday can fade today and disappear tomorrow.

For the child, it's the nice plaything, the warm fuzzy to hold and cuddle or the bright bauble to manipulate and delight in.

Time passes, and the toys are put away. Now it's the newest thing in clothes, the fancy sports car, the latest aspect of pop culture, the exciting date, visions and dreams of what may be, and school.

Time passes, and school is over. The date becomes a marriage, there is a home, and there is work to be done. Now it's the economic struggle, the social circle, responsibility, deadlines to be met.

Time passes, and work is done. One by one, old friends slip away, and it seems the world has changed. Now it's the struggle to maintain identity, to be occupied, to keep alive and stay in touch.

Thus, all through a lifetime the change goes on, with new values forever crowding out the old. One by one, and each in turn, the importances of former times give way to new ones coming on. Their comings and goings relate directly to the times and circumstances of our lives.

In this ever-changing continuum, then, is there no value that endures? Is there nothing that underlies, nothing that ties it all together? There is: for you see, in this lifelong scale of values there is one unidentified constant to which all the others are merely incidental. This is *life itself*. Herein resides the lasting and ultimate value.

Happiness Isn't a Given

A song often heard along about the first of January contains this line: "God bless you and send you a happy new year." It's a nice sentiment, I suppose, but there are at least three things wrong with it.

First: God doesn't *send* happiness. God may send the stuff of which happiness may be made, but it's up to us to take that stuff and make the happiness ourselves. Some do, and some don't.

Second: God doesn't send anything *by the year*. Life comes in smaller pieces than this; it is more momentary than annual. Its happiness quotient doesn't usually rise and fall by the year, but by the episode, and episodes can be no longer than a twinkle. As happiness is measured, an instant can be momentous.

Third: Not *everything* that comes is sent by God anyway. For example, some things that come arise out of our own past, materializing sometimes like ghosts to haunt us, sometimes like beneficent genies to help us. Some things that come are the maturing fruits of seeds we planted long ago. Of course, there are other sources, too.

So I would say: God bless you and grant you, if it be a proper gift, another year of time, and along with this gift of time as pleasant a mix as possible of the stuff of which happiness can be made. Then I would leave it to you to receive and accept all this material gratefully and use it well.

A Constitutional Issue

The body politic called the United States of America is constituted in a certain way, and this way of being constituted is made a matter of record in a document we call the Constitution. If an action taken within the body politic does not conform to the way that body is constituted, we say the action is unconstitutional, and usually this decision is made by the Supreme Court of the nation.

The human body is also constructed in a certain way. For instance, if arsenic is taken into it, that is unconstitutional, and the body suffers. The body is not constituted to tolerate a great deal of arsenic. If, for instance, the body is caused to fall a thousand feet onto a stone pavement, it dies, for the body is not constituted to survive a shock of such magnitude. Whatever is incompatible with the bodily constitution is destructive of the body.

However, we human beings are more than body; we know this, do we not? We are also mind, soul, spirit. It is in spirit as well as body that we are constituted in a certain way; human life is constitutional. Some things will conform, and others will be incompatible.

Our thinkings and our doings can be constitutional, or they can prove to be unconstitutional. We have no Supreme Court to decide for us which is which; one way or another, we must find out for ourselves. Sooner or later we do; we discover that some things work and some don't.

Often, however, we are slow to learn or, having learned, slow to put our lessons into practice. We ought to know by now, for instance, that loving is more constitutional with us than hating is. We ought to understand by now that when we try to make our life work in unconstitutional ways we are soon in trouble. Sometimes these troubles are psychological, sometimes they are physical, and sometimes they are both.

Take our sexuality for example. It is an aspect of our constitution, and when we use it in unconstitutional ways we always get hurt, sometimes in subtle ways we do not easily identify. Often, however, the consequences are not subtle at all; sometimes, as a result of our sexual misuses, we get sick and sometimes we die.

Concepts of sin and judgment appear to be simply a theological representation of this profound fact: If we violate the way our life is designed to function, we suffer for it. Entertaining incompatibles proves destructive.

Those who will not ask concerning a thing "Is it right?" might well ask "Is it constitutional?" Honestly considered, in any instance the two questions will yield identical answers. The bottom line appears to be this: The nearer we can bring our lives into harmony with the way they are constituted to work, the more fulfilled and the more whole we will be.

THE SOUL'S DEEP AND SECRET DREAM

My soul has been an eagle seeking heights,
    a lily upborne on slender stem seeking light,
    an orphan child looking for its kin.

My soul has been a questing soul,
    longing, probing, far-ranging, reaching,
    straining at the edge of things,
    soaring high as flesh would let it go.

All of that was preliminary to this.

Goes forth now my venturing soul
    on this one ultimate quest—
The bounds are broken, the tether's severed,
    let loose, I venture on.

Comes now the freedom my soul long sought,
    to search the deeps,
    to seek new worlds
    and truth beyond the reach of mind.

Comes fulfillment now at last
    of the soul's deep and secret dream.

Images We Make

Well over two thousand years ago, describing his ideal state of human affairs, Greek philosopher Plato wrote, "Their children will not grow up amid images of deformity." This statement deserves careful scrutiny and has particular relevancy in our western world in our time.

The way in which it rears its children is a valid test of any civilization. Actually, there cannot be a better one. Plato understood this.

He also understood that as our children grow up they are shaped according to their impressions of the world around them. There can be exceptions, but they are rare. The chief interest of all the young is to become adult. They want to catapult themselves into the adult world as quickly as possible. Whether with dolls or guns, children play adult roles in their games. Two drives move them: to know what the adult world is like and to imitate it.

Children and youth want to understand; they want to see. They are image seekers. We around them may not realize that they are image seekers, but to them it is very real: Whether we know it or not, we are image makers.

What sort of images are we making? Are they true to life, or are they distorted pictures of what life is like? There is, for instance, something we call an "adult motion picture." Our young, of course, want to know what it is like. Finding out, they say, "So that's the adult world." There is something called an "adult book store," a store especially for adults. What is special about it? Finding out, our young say, "Ah, this is how it is to be adult." Should we then be surprised if our young people point their lives in this direction?

By means of our media and otherwise, are we showing our young a true cross section of current life or mainly a dark underside of it? I fear it is mostly the aberrations of our society, not its more stable mainstream, that we serve up for the image-hungry to feed upon. If we persist in creating and parading images of deformity, should we be surprised if our children suffer the very deformities we have pictured for them?

Yes, of course, the prevailing themes of literature, art, and news reporting must of necessity be that which is extraordinary. But why must the emphasis be on the extraordinarily ugly, mean, cheap, and vulgar? Why not give more attention to the extraordinarily beautiful, noble, heroic, and lofty? The implications here are shameful.

The images we make are worshiped most by the most fragile and the most impressionable among us, our children. I fear we are doing too much of what Plato would shun, creating "images of deformity." Such images can accurately represent marginal elements and dark undersides of society, but they surely do not represent the mainstream of adult life. But do our children know this? And don't you think we ought to tell them?

Our Walk in the Garden: A Parable

You know the gate in the east garden wall—
  The one with the white arched trellis
And the honeysuckle vine,
  Where the eucalyptus stands stately tall?
I will come at nine.

Please be waiting there
  And in gown of morning blue.
The moon should be rising, and new,
  A silver crescent in the evening sky,
And a few bright stars standing by.
  There and then I'll come to you.

I'll take your hand and you'll take mine,
  And we'll walk the garden through,
Down the path where the roses grow
  And the columbine.
And we'll stand by the lily pond
  In the moon's dim glow,
And stroll through the Grecian colonnade
  Where ancient ivies twine,
And across the little stone bridge.

Remember the carved-marble love seat
  That stands stone-white on the other side?
There we'll sit a while.
  Hearing the cricket serenade,
The garden symphony, as the gentle breeze
  Caresses lightly the live oak trees.

It is beautiful here.

But we will rise,
  Gaze for one last time to the arching sky,
And together we'll walk the cobble path
  Winding down to the western gate,
And there, my darling, we'll say good bye.

THE RESPONSIBILITY OF BEING FREE

Suppose I want something, and this thing I want I cannot create or produce for myself. If I am to have it, it must come to me from others. I cannot buy it, steal it, borrow it, or in any other way obtain it by act of my will. If it is to be mine, I must receive it as a gift.

I do have this gift. It is freedom, and I have it at two levels of my experience. First, I have the freedom that nature or divine Providence has provided me—the freedom to open my hand or to make a fist, the freedom to help another up from the dust or to strike another down, the freedom to possess my powers in discipline or to fling them wantonly to the winds. This freedom came as a birthday gift, my very first. I think it can best be defined as a gift from God.

My other freedom came as a gift from other persons of my kind, people who often sacrificed and sometimes died that I might have it. By reason of this freedom, I can vote in my country's elections, I can speak as I wish, I can choose my vocation, I can own property, I can move about at will.

These are my two freedoms, gifts to me, the one by a kind Providence and the other by heroic persons who have come and gone before. I am convinced that these, human and divine, who provided my freedoms for me, have trusted that I will use these freedoms well. If I have any sense of responsibility at all, I must see myself as under some obligation. I am trusted; and I should prove myself most ungrateful ever to betray this trust.

All things considered, I feel I must accept the obligation my freedoms place upon me. I must understand, as someone has said, that freedom does not give me a license to do as I please, but the liberty to do as I ought. I must understand that freedom is a treasure to be preserved and passed on, not to be squandered and therefore lost to all who will follow. I must understand that I have no right, in the name of freedom, to choose a way of life that, if everybody chose, would destroy freedom itself and be the ruin of us all. I must understand that freedom in itself is neither good nor bad, but is given character by the use I make of it.

My freedoms are my highest privilege. They provide me a breadth of opportunity as limitless as my time and strength will allow. They constitute a wide arena in which I can move and express myself. They are my life's most precious asset.

My freedoms are also my greatest stewardship. My management of them is a daily obligation for as many days as life is long. How I use them is the most critical issue I will ever face. It is by my use of freedom that I will rise to inspiring heights, or descend into abysmal deeps, or settle somewhere in between. It is from this freedom stuff that I can fashion wings for soaring or make a stone to sink me.

Shall we set our sights on soaring, you and I? Why not? Can we remember and be encouraged by this: For soaring, no wings are ever more sure than those that are most mature, those feathered by long time and made strong by many flights.

The Marbles We Hold

A doting mother took her small son to meet a great man. Smiling down at the little fellow, the man extended his right hand. The mother noted with embarrassment that the boy responded with his left.

Attempting a correction, she said, "Give the man your right hand, son." "I can't," the boy replied. "And why can't you?" asked the mother. Her son answered, "Because that's the hand that has my marbles in it."

Well, small children aren't the only people among us who have marbles in our hands. We bigger people sometimes also have ours. Like that small boy, holding onto our trinkets, we often deny ourselves the larger privilege.

There are the possessions we outwardly hold, and there are the attitudes and fixations we hold within. How frequently these stand between us and the better things we really want! Clutching our marbles, we don't open our hands to receive the better gifts.

I may lift up my hands, imploring God. However, holding marbles, that is terribly difficult, for the uplifted hand with marbles in it must be a closed hand, therefore a fist. It's very difficult for me to clasp the hand of another unless I open mine. Of course, if I open it, my marbles will fall out.

Well, let them go.

How Much Are You Worth?

Ask concerning any man, "What's he worth?" and you are likely to receive a financial report. The question, however, is one of many-layered meanings.

In the labor market, a man's worth may be measured on par with a horse: How much can he do in an hour? In the business arena, he may be valued alongside a machine: How useful is he to those who purchase his skills?

His higher worth, however, must be measured in terms of personal relationship. For example, here was Roger, thirty-one years of age, one of six thousand citizens of his community, husband of a young wife, father of a four-your-old son, Boy Scout leader, member of his church's choir. Suddenly he lost his life in an industrial accident. How much was Roger worth? He was worth much to many—the total incalculable.

Yes, of course there is a lot of the mundane about living. A man comes into this world with no teeth, with not much hair, and with eyes that won't focus, and if he remains very long in the world, he will likely leave it with no teeth, not much hair, and eyes that won't focus! But this isn't the whole story. Between the coming and the going a lot of living can be done, and in the course of it, life will touch life in many and varied ways. And the worth of it all will never be known.

Yes, it's a big world, with many people and a long history. Nevertheless, nobody ever comes into it but that it is changed at least a little and sometimes a great deal. Everybody makes a difference. Sometimes that difference can be no greater than the change in sea level when a pebble is dropped in, but sometimes it is as though the ocean overflows.

How much are you worth? Who knows? No one knows now, and no one ever will. Your financial assets can be easily computed and totaled, but your personal worth cannot be recorded on the final line of a ledger page. Human worth is not numerical, to be measured and recorded in digits. Human worth is personal and is recorded only in terms of meaning in the lives of other persons over the whole length of a lifetime and who can measure that?

Therefore, if you ever come to a downtime when it seems your life isn't worth much, factor in all the rest of it—all the sixty or seventy or eighty or ninety years of it. This will add up to a total that even you will never know. The worth of life, you see, is not to be computed by the moment, but by the lifetime.

The Human Advantage

If a man builds his house out of plumb, the law of gravitation will pull it down, and the more it leans the more quickly it falls. But if a man builds his house plumb, that same law will help hold it up. Suppose he builds of stone. The law of gravitation will pull each stone snugly down atop the stone beneath and hold it there. It isn't even necessary that the builder use cement to hold the stones together; the law of gravitation will do this for him.

Thus, the same law that will destroy the man's house if he builds one way will preserve it for him if he builds another. If he builds in conformity with the way the law works, he is helped. If he builds otherwise, he suffers for it.

So it is with the ways we live. As there are laws that govern nature, there are laws that govern human life. These are not arbitrarily imposed somehow from without, but are actually built into us as aspects of what we are. Deep within, they quietly wait, and, like all laws, their force is not much felt until a violation occurs; it is then they spring into action.

As the law of gravitation will pronounce judgment upon the builder whose house leans, so do the laws of life deal with us when we're out of line. Of course, a leaning house can stand a long while before coming down. Likewise, we who are out of kilter with life can get by for time, but at length a vigilant inner monitor will make its presence and power felt.

The law of gravitation is a friendly law, helping us more than we imagine, I suspect. Without it, we humans would be unable even to have a home for ourselves on this planet. It is by the law of gravitation that we are able to stand up and walk rather than float away, but if we step over a precipice it is this very law that will pull us down.

In similar manner, the laws of life are friendly laws, existing to guide us to higher levels of development, attainment, and self-realization and fulfillment. They never annoy us unless we have offended them.

All this means that we humans have an enormous advantage, one that lesser animals apparently do not have. Ours is the advantage of a built-in guidance system that points us forever forward and nudges us when we go astray. Traditionally, it has been called the moral law. But by whatever name called, or called by no name at all, it is there; indelibly and inescapably, it is there. Nor can anyone, of whatever qualification, hope to be excused from its authority.

The laws that govern life do not mean to limit or imprison us, but to help us achieve what we may and to guide us ever upward toward the summits we are meant to reach. Think of it: In all these years of our ongoing lives, you and I have been blessed with this enormous advantage, a blessing we still have and always will.

Assurance

Be it strongly said here once again:
 However dark or long the night
 Comes at length the morning light—
 And so it has ever been.

Write it clear that all can see:
 Whatever storm may cloud the day,
 Some wind sometime will drive it all away—
 And so it will ever be.

Book of Prior Knowledge

Yes, we can learn by experience—by trial and error, by starts and stops, by blundering into dead-end alleys and trying to find our way out again. But there is another way: we can learn from the experiences of others.

There is, for example, the rule book that comes with the game. If I am to use those cards or blocks or other doodads as they are designed to be used and in ways to give most pleasure, I am well advised to consider the rule book.

There is the book of assembly instruction that comes with Junior's little red wagon, and unless I am prepared to make a real mess of things, I'd better observe what it says.

There is the road atlas that I can use as I drive through country I've never seen before. Others have been there ahead of me, and in this book they are giving me the benefit of what they have found out about these roads.

There is the recipe book on the kitchen shelf, information assembled by someone who has tried and tested methods of food preparation, and has made for me a record of what works well and what doesn't.

There is the operator's manual that comes with the machine I buy, and if I am to flip the right switches and pull the proper levers to make the thing work as it's supposed to, I would be stupid indeed to consign this book to the trash can.

These small books are all alike in one respect: each is a *Book of Prior Knowledge*. All of them are telling me what somebody else has already learned; they save me the necessity of blundering around until I find out the hard way; they spare me sundry mistakes and endless frustration.

Well, our life comes with a *Book of Prior Knowledge*. There are a million volumes of it, more or less. Some are in print, and some are in the lives of persons who have traveled this way before. It is a majestic work, this book, compiled as it was over many long centuries and the product of countless contributors. Of course, we can find in it chapters like "Grandma's Recipe for Clam Chowder," but we'll also find others such as "The Ten Commandments," "The Magna Carta," "The Sermon on the Mount," and the poems of Robert Browning.

This great book can tell us much about putting the pieces together to make of our life the whole thing it is meant to be. It can spare us the trauma of straying into many dark alleys we otherwise would, and of following paths that lead only into some dreary morass or some abysmal deep.

Why should we go bumbling along, learning costly lessons that all the while are available to us at no cost at all? Why should we go stumbling into pits that have been clearly marked with warning flags for a thousand years? Why should we go blunderingly on, making the very mistakes that have proven to be folly again and again?

The accumulated wisdom of the ages is open to us. It might just help us more than we know if we should respectfully pause and honestly seek the counsel it offers.

You see, we don't have to try everything to know that some things won't work. Thanks to a small chapter in this enormous compendium of prior knowledge, we already now that arsenic is poison. At least, by now, we ought to know. We ought to know by now that some of our so-called lifestyles are actually death warrants. We ought to know by now that it's only the high roads that do not dead-end at last, that only the high roads lead at length to beauty.

THE TWO FACES OF DISCONTENT

The world owes much to its discontented. Discontent has been the spark that has lit most of the refining fires that have served to purge and cleanse what was needed among humankind. There are, however, two kinds of discontent.

First, there is the kind that *works*. It puts its shoulder to the wheel and tries to move things up a little, and it has served us well. It has often inspired us by its passion for improvement and its pursuit of ideals.

Second, there is the discontent that expects *other people to work*. This is the demanding kind that insists that other people could easily fix everything if only they would. Usually, it is quick to fix blame for the inequities it perceives and to assign responsibility for correcting them.

This second variety of discontent can do dramatic and even destructive things to get attention, uttering shrill cries to make its demand heard. It is usually quite selective of the issues it will choose to be discontented about. As though even the smallest of thorny thickets must be cleared away by next Thursday, it often tries to make big issues out of minor matters. Its demand is that whatever it finds disagreeable be modified to its liking.

Shrill discontent, however, tends to ignore certain basic truths. One of these is this: Life almost always has some of the disagreeable about it, and most of us learn to live with this in some reasonable measure of equanimity. The fact is that life comes with a built-in element of struggle, and to be discontented with this is to reject the very character of life itself.

Persons who chronically complain about the nuances of time and circumstance need to understand that the times are always hard for those who require that life be always easy.

This Voice We Hear

So it's a hard world to be a dreamer in?
　　Do you suppose that I do not know?
I was there, and I was a dreamer, too;
　　I am there, and I dream along with you.

Think you that you are the first to know,
　　To feel the sharp, hot shaft of pain?
I felt it long ago.

You complain of thorns and bitter wine;
　　You say you have a cross to bear!
Shall I tell you of mine?

Hostile voices wildly shout and cry!
　　Trickster voices are whispering in the night!
The word I heard was "Crucify!"

Postgraduate Lessons

Why does it take so long to learn elemental truths we should have known from the start? Too bad that it does! What grief we could spare ourselves if we only understood early some of the life principles it usually takes us most of a lifetime to discover! For instance, there before us at the beginning, as in all these ensuing years, were the lessons to be learned from the common lichen. Think about it:

Two thallophytes, fungus and alga, can form a co-op, living together in symbiotic association, mutually sustaining each other. The result is a lichen. Lichens are a large family of variously shaped and colored organisms that live in virtually every part of the world.

Under favorable circumstances, both fungi and algae are able to live independently. Under other conditions, however, neither could possibly survive alone. In these situations, the two often get together, fuse their very bodies into one body, and so become a lichen. We can find lichens growing on wood and stone and earth all the way from the Equator to the Arctic.

A lichen is about 90 percent fungi and 10 percent algae, and these constitute its entire being. A fungus, being devoid of chlorophyll, cannot produce its own food, but an alga can. And so it does, producing the food, not only for itself, but also for its companion. It would be unable to do this, however, except the fungus provide the necessary water and carbon dioxide.

Thus, between the two of them, the fungus and the alga have a really good thing going. By their mutual interdependence, they can occupy habitats where neither could exist without the other. They can exist only because they work together, and by their cooperative effort they reconstitute themselves into a single living thing.

With such intimacy, do you suppose there is ever any trouble between them? Do they ever argue or have compatibility problems? Do they suffer from jealousy or selfishness or resentment? Apparently not; they get along splendidly together. Consider how they do it:

The fungus supplies the essential ingredients, and the alga uses its power of photosynthesis to make their food. The alga is able to maintain this power because the fungus provides moisture to prevent dehydration. It appears that division of labor is never a problem between them. Nor does either ever say to the other, "That's not fair" or "You're not doing your share" or "You're expecting too much of me."

It never happens, but Fungus might say to Alga, "Little fellow, we fungi have you outnumbered nine to one. You are a minority; and because we are the majority, you must do as we say." I doubt, too, that Alga ever says to

Fungus, "Have a heart, you monster; we algae deserve a fair handicap in this game; because we are numerically disadvantaged, we deserve some special consideration."

It is clear that neither party in this symbiosis is of a suspicious nature or critical disposition. Neither demands special privilege or is unwilling to assume some responsibility. Neither is looking for a fault to find in the other or a way to pass its own blame on to somebody else. The two of them know that they need each other and are willing to leave it there.

Aren't you glad you have discovered these truths? Don't you wish everybody had?

Never Close the Unopened Door

There is an ancient and honored story about an important citizen who once prepared a fine banquet and invited many. All sent regrets: one man had bought land and needed to go to examine it, another had bought five yoke of oxen. So the excuses went. One by one, the invited ones excused themselves right out of high privilege and fine opportunity.

I don't know why. No doubt, however, their excuses were one thing and their real reasons another. Maybe some weren't willing to commit themselves to a specific appointment, wanting rather to reserve the time to use as most pleased them at the moment. Maybe some felt uncomfortable accepting the hospitality of the big house they had so resentfully complained about. Maybe some didn't want to accept the generosity of the rich man, lest they later feel some obligation to him. Maybe some looked upon what was free as suspect, being convinced that such generosity must certainly have a self-serving motive somewhere about it.

No, I don't know why the invited didn't accept, but I do have a good idea of what they missed. They didn't see the festooned hall, the plush tapestries, the burning candles, or the face of the pleased host as they came. They didn't hear the orchestra or the singing or the voice of their host saying welcome. They didn't taste the fine food or touch the outstretched hand of the good man who stood at the door to greet them. They didn't enjoy the good fellowship of the festive gathering. They missed all of this.

But worse, much worse, they never knew what they missed; they never gave themselves a chance to find out. Preoccupied with their own small worlds, they didn't allow themselves even a glimpse of a larger one. They paced off their little fields and groomed their new-bought oxen until the sun went down and it was too dark to see.

Although the grand portal of the house on the hill stood wide open to them, their minds were closed against it. There are two ways to close a door and two who can close it. It may be closed by the one who keeps the key and who can thus deny admission to any who may seek it. Or it may be closed, though standing fully open, by the one who declines to enter by it. The one type of closing is as effective as the other.

In our minds we are perpetually opening and closing doors; and when we close a door against the unknown or the untried, we shut off the very possibility that, for us, this door will ever open at all. If we close doors against life's finer invitations, we deny ourselves great privilege and then have no way of ever knowing how much we really missed.

Each new day comes with a new invitation—a parchment scroll, engraved, with bright red ribbons on it. It is an invitation to life, another day of it. So, with firm hand, fling wide the door and walk with confidence in. Look about with seeing eyes and drink in the beauty of the festooned hall, the aroma of candles burning, the light of sumptuous tables spread. *Live* another day!

Is There Any Wind?

The aged seaman and the young novice stand together at the dock, admiring the young man's new sailboat. The day is clear and there before them lies the calm and gently rolling sea.

The younger man says to the older, "Do you think there's any wind?" The older replies, "I'm not sure, son. Sometimes it's hard to tell; but you have only to hoist a sail, and then you will know."

A truth both exciting and profound is here expressed. It is a truth that holds not only at a seaside dock, but also for all of us when we stand at any juncture in our life's ongoing journey. Sometimes we just can't know about the winds until we hoist a sail and see what will happen. Saying this another way, we don't know what resources we may have for any task until we undertake it.

There is the amusing but thought-provoking story about a question put to a somewhat simpleminded fellow: "Can you play the fiddle?" His answer: "I don't know; I've never tried." As far as this fellow was concerned, he might well have been the world's best fiddler; he just hadn't found out yet!

Suppose da Vinci had never taken up a brush or put paint to canvas. We never would have known, would we, how great a painter was in him just waiting to come out. Nor would he have known. We never know, do we, what powers are in us until we put ourselves to the test.

This we can do by choice, perhaps undertaking some hazardous venture that calls for courage. Then, too, sometimes the testing is forced upon us by trying circumstances we would never have chosen. In either instance, however, we are likely to discover within us powers that, without the testing, we would never have known were there.

In the ongoing ventures of life, early or late, whatever the issues we must deal with, the critical question is this: Do we have what it takes? Well, we'll never know until we try. Is there any wind? It can indeed be hard to tell; but we must never be afraid to find out. We have only to hoist a sail, and then we'll know.

Part VII

Our Summons to the Summits

It's very difficult to explore the heights unless we are willing to do some climbing. It is easy enough to stand in the valley and speculate about what may be up there. It is even easier to stand in the valley and declare that there is nothing worth going for. But we'll never know for sure until we wear the scrapes and bruises that come from having tried.

If a towering ideal looms against our sky, we can be sure it will not come down to us. If we are to meet it, we must buckle on our climbing gear and turn our faces to the summit.

Ideals are not much given to compromise; they are wholly unwilling to meet us halfway. Should they consent to accommodate our fears, our lassitude, or our timidity, they would lose the very quality that gives them ideal status. It is not in their nature to surrender their identity to our indifference.

Nor are they content to have us adore them from afar. They do not seek only to be admired. Ideals seek incarnation, to come alive in human flesh and mind and spirit. Their appearance is a call to action; from their place at the summit, they call us to don our climbing togs and make for the heights.

Yes, the time may come when age or arthritis will prevent an attempt at Mount McKinley, but such limitation can never shackle the spirit.

The Risks Love Takes

For love of country and comrades in the battle, a soldier rushes bravely into a danger far greater than mere duty calls for him to face. For love of her child, a mother plunges into the flames that engulf her house.

Such people are heroes or heroines, moved by love to do heroic deeds. But there are other heroes too—less spectacular their doings but no less valorous—common folk in the common ventures of life who love and give and reach out and risk.

A young woman marries, gives herself away in a lifetime contract, for better or for worse, for whatever happens. All that her womanhood is and means she lays on the line. Will this man be worthy of the gift she gives? Her heart ventures out, goes forth to him; will he receive it gently? There is risk in what the young woman does, great risk. Why does she take the risk? Because she loves; and loving, she doesn't think much about the risk.

A young man marries, and he takes a risk. He obligates his whole life, pledges all his years, all he is and all he can be. He promises to love and to cherish. What will happen? Actually, he scarcely knows this girl, but he loves her. Because he does, he gives, and he doesn't think much about the risk.

The young couple longs for a child to lavish their love upon. They take a risk. Will the baby be normal, or will the miracle of birth somehow snarl somewhere as it sometimes does? But love is overwhelming, and these two think little of the risk.

Then comes the child—beautiful, delightful, full of promise—and love must be prepared to suffer a little and maybe a lot. Whenever there is a frightened cry in the night or the fever rises, love hurts a little. There comes a time when, to teach a better way, a parent must administer a discipline, and love suffers a lot. Or the child is ungrateful, disrespectful, disloyal, and love is deeply pained.

Years go by (how quickly they go), and the child is adult now. Love has done all that love can do, hoped all that love could hope, dreamed all that love could dream. And now? Is love's dream fulfilled? Sometimes yes, and there is joy. Sometimes no, and love hurts and hurts and hurts and goes right on loving.

Oh, the risks that love takes! How heroic love is! How fragile a thing to be so brave! How easily wounded! How slow to die!

THE HIGH COST OF LIVING

"The cost of living" is a phrase much used these days. Something called the cost of living index is a major concern in national affairs. By cost of living we mean the amount of money we must spend for food, fuel, housing, clothing, and personal necessities.

Actually, however, these and other similar items are only the incidentals; the whole cost of living is much greater. I cannot give you the numbers by the month or the year, but I can give you the bottom line: In the end, our living will cost us everything.

When the bills are all in, when the final settlements are made and the books closed, the tally will show that we have used up everything we had. All will be gone somewhere beyond our reach—all we have inherited and earned, all our strength and talent and time. All spent, we will be done with it—finished.

If the much-discussed cost of living is of concern to us, the *high* cost is even more so. This cost is higher even than we might like to think. Ultimately, our living will cost us even life itself. In a very real sense, living is the chief cause of death. A man dies, and someone asks, "What killed him?" Well, living did it. He lived (at least as far as this world is concerned) until his life was all used up. He spent what he had until it was all gone. Maybe he avoided tuberculosis and polio; maybe he won a bout with cancer and recovered from pneumonia; but living did him in at last. One way or another, sooner or later, it always does.

It is true, not only that we die from having lived, but also that we die from what we have lived *for*. If we have lived exclusively for ourselves, nothing is left, or certainly not much anyway. To the extent we have lived for others, something remains—possibly a very great deal. If I squander all of my life's resources on me, they end when I die, but if I invest them in others and in values that really matter, they can continue in perpetuity.

Perhaps the primary privilege of our human life is to transform time and energy and talent into personal and spiritual qualities that have survival power, both in ourselves and in those we leave behind. How to beat the high cost of living? I can think of no better way.

Walkers and Gropers

Two men walk on Main Street, and both are blind. One gropes his way, face down-turned in contortions of dread, hands outstretched in wild motions of search, feet doubtfully shuffling as though they mistrust even one another.

The other strides, a bit of a spring in his step, his head held high in the posture of one who sees, his white cane tapping lightly before him as he goes, the sound like music on the walkway.

One walker and one groper. The walker may stumble sometimes, and he may suffer bruises now and then. He may carry a scar from having bumped into a lamppost a day or so ago, and tomorrow he may bump into another. But he will stand up and walk. If today he stumbles at a broken curb, tomorrow he will stand up and walk again.

The groper, afraid of what is in his dark, is so in dread of stumbling that he never really walks. Thinking of every step as a potential disaster, he never picks up a foot but slides it tentatively forward, as though, should he pick it up, he might never find a place to put it down again.

To both men the darkness is alike, for neither can see. As you and I move into our future, neither can we. Some of us are walkers and some are gropers. The difference is due, not to something in our darkness, but to something within ourselves.

In our minds, we give character to the unknown. In our imaginations, we populate the regions where we haven't yet gone; we people our darkness. In our blindness, what we see as being there shows itself in every step we take.

Outgrowing the Infantile

Among humans, the road from infancy to maturity is not a straight line forward; it involves, in fact, some 180-degree turns.

We start out, most of us, being loved. Before we are truly mature we must move from being loved to loving. In the beginning, we are surrounded by those who love us, who lavish their loving care upon us. It's their loving that sees us through our helpless years. At last we are on our own. What happens then? We who have been loved so much should be loving now; it's our turn.

We start out, most of us, as recipients. All around us are those who give us care, whose attention we receive moment by moment; they never leave us alone. We are on someone's mind every hour of every day and night. Our smallest cry brings someone running to attend us. Before we can even talk we are talked to; others whisper gentle words and sing for us little songs. We receive our daily baths and our baby's milk; we are forever receiving. But if we are ever to be mature, we must graduate from receiving into giving.

We start out, all of us, as totally dependent. A newborn calf will rise to its feet and walk alongside its mother. But we don't; we depend on others for everything. We do not feed or clothe ourselves; others will keep us warm or cool; others will do for us all that is done. From our very first, we are wholly and helplessly dependent. But if we are ever to reach maturity, we must move from being dependent to being dependable, trustworthy, responsible.

We start out, all of us, being persistently acquisitive. As soon as we discover our hands, we begin to reach for things, and adults soon learn to keep small objects beyond our reach. Whatever it is, we want it. Unless carefully guarded by someone wiser, we will even put it into our mouths, as though to make it a veritable part of what we are. To mature, we must outgrow our childish acquisitiveness; we must move over into generosity.

Yes, at our beginnings we are egocentric, aren't we? We don't value others for who they are nearly as much as we value them for what they can do for us. If they entertain us and give us our food and a lot of attention, we like them. In true maturity, however, this changes; we no longer value others according to the ways they serve us so much as we value them for their own intrinsic worth. Maturing is the process of moving from the egocentric to the altruistic.

Some of us, however, are slow to mature, and some of us never do. At age forty we can be infants still. One who expects to be loved but never loves is surely immature. One who wants always to receive but never give hasn't really grown up yet. To shun the responsibility that belongs with adulthood is to perpetuate the dependency of the infant child. One who at age forty, with rarely a generous thought, grasps at everything within reach is simply an infant of larger size.

The bottom line is this: Along with the adventure of growing bigger and older, we can enjoy the even greater adventure of outgrowing our baby ways. To do so is what it means to reach maturity. What a blessing—to have all these years to work at it!

A DECISION'S OTHER HALF

How should we make a decision? Well, make it, *all* of it. Sometimes we make only the first half of a decision. But when we make our decisions by halves, we make misery for ourselves.

It is useful to understand what we actually do when we decide. The "cisions" are a fascinating family of words. "Cision" means "to cut." *INcision* is a cutting *into*, as a surgeon does when he or she operates. *CIRCUMcision* is a cutting *around*, as is done in removing the foreskin from the penis of a male child. *DEcision* is a cutting *off*, as when in choosing one road we cut off all the others.

Our trouble is that we often choose a road without cutting the others off. We keep on thinking too much about how it might have been had we gone some other way.

Consider the fellow, for instance, who goes to the altar with a girl and then spends the rest of his life dreaming about how it might have been had he married another. It scarcely needs saying that this sort of ambivalence doesn't make for the happiest of marriages.

Or consider the man who accepts employment with an industrial firm and then is forever looking over the fence and thinking of the position he might have had somewhere else. Certainly, this state of mind cannot be expected to produce the best of working relationships.

Or consider the family in the process of purchasing a house. At last they choose the one at 717 Park Street. They move in, but they keep talking about the fine features of the house they almost bought, the one over on Wishbone Avenue. If they are ever to settle down and enjoy 717 Park Street, they'll be well advised to forget they ever saw the house on Wishbone.

Robert Frost wrote of two roads that "diverged in a yellow wood," and of a traveler who was sorry he "could not travel both." In any particular aspect of our living, each can travel only one road at a time. Again and again, at various intersections and junctions along the way, we must choose which we will take.

But that choice is only the first half of the decision. The other half is to give up all other roads, to cut them off. Having done this, we can sit back and relax and be somewhat contented where we are.

Voices from Within

We humans are born seven pounds and twenty inches of possibility. The years pass, and we change with the passing. In the course of time, the seven pounds become one hundred and fifty and the twenty inches five-feet-ten. Physically, we grow.

It's virtually automatic that we do so. Given normal conditions, it just happens. Yes, of course, we can stunt our growth with drugs, alcohol, nicotine, and in various other ways. But assuming the body is provided proper food, drink, and care, we grow up in physical stature.

The physical is very apparent and quite demanding. We know it well: labor and rest, eating and earning, waking and sleeping, sight and sound, injury and pain, time and decay. We need nobody to call our attention to the fact that life is physical: cut a finger and it hurts; go days without food and the stomach protests in pain. Our bodies have their ways of reminding us that they are real.

All the while, as the body lives and grows, it keeps us informed as to its state of being. From time to time the foot says, "Hey, you, I need a bigger shoe; I'm hurting in this one." Sooner or later, we are able to see over walls that once seemed so high. Thus do our bodies keep telling us about their needs and their conditions.

On occasion, however, another voice can be heard—this voice a whisper maybe, and perhaps more felt than heard. We may hear it when standing at the newly made grave of one we have loved, or in the glow of a glorious sunset, or when great music swells in crescendo, or in a time of meditation or prayer.

We do not comprehend all dimensions of our life by weighing and measuring. The physical is only part of it. There is also spirit.

Of course, the spiritual doesn't make itself as felt as does the physical. In the contest between the physical and the spiritual for our attention, the physical has the advantage. Hunger, thirst, pain, fatigue, heat, and cold—these speak loudly, each in a language of its own, each in a language we readily understand.

The needs and hungering of the spirit, although just as real, are not so vocal. To hear these voices, we must exercise our inner sensibilities and listen with greater care. Neglected, the stomach will shout protest, but a starved heart has no voice for shouting. Unlike the foot, the soul has no way to protest the restraints that hinder its growth. A hungering spirit scarcely whimpers but slowly wastes away, and usually we don't understand what is happening.

We ought to know, without their telling us, that our inner selves need some beauty, some love, some light. Our souls need nurture; they need us to send them some elevated thoughts to feed upon. If we are to maintain them in health, we must carefully protect them from the poisons that destroy and the parasites that would steal their life away.

As much as our outward ones, our inner lives need our attention. It is needful that we cultivate an ear for hearing the voices that whisper from within.

YOU CAN!

If I might assemble the millions of American youth in a single place and have their attention for five minutes, what should I say to them? Out of the observation and experience of my many years, what should I say to these who have virtually all their years yet ahead? Without doubt, there are many things I should say, but here is one thing I would: "Young man, young woman, don't listen to anyone who says you can't!"

If you were born of humble parentage, live in a substandard house, and have very little money, some will say you haven't a chance to achieve very much in life. Don't you believe it! Others have, and you can!

That mind of yours is yours, you know, and you can develop it as you will. It is you who will determine the course you will take, in what direction you will aim your life. You can let others set the compass for you, or you can set your own; the choice is yours.

If yours is a rundown neighborhood, and if the youth you know are street-corner incorrigibles, some will say that you are destined to a career in crime. Don't you believe it; others have risen above such circumstances, and so can you.

You are not a puppet, able to move only as somebody else pulls your strings. You can decide some things for yourself; you don't have to wait for others to initiate everything. Your life is yours, you know; you are nobody's slave; you have freedom; use it.

You are not a jellyfish, able only to take the shape of whatever situation you are in. Neither are you a lump of lifeless clay, held helplessly in the hands of others to be molded as they design. You can assert yourself; you can say yes or you can say no; you choose.

You are not a roadside stone, condemned always to be what you now are. You can think, and you can dream, and you can aspire. You can look up; and when you do, you will see some stars. They will call to you, and something in you will rise to meet them.

You are not an animal-thing, scrounging husks that others may leave; you don't have to live on leftovers. You are a human person with all the qualities of personhood anyone ever had. You are uniquely you; there has never been another, nor will there ever be. There is a place in the world for you. If you don't fill it, no one ever will.

Yes, you can; don't listen to anybody who says you can't. Yes indeed, there may be rough road to travel, mountains that are hard to climb, obstacles along the way. But you are not the first to have traveled here. Others have and have made it through. So can you.

The end can justify the journey. Turn now to face the heights, take a deep breath, and start!

A Choice of Masters

Members of the orchestra sit or stand about on stage messing with their instruments—tuning violins, tapping on drums, blowing into horns, strumming on strings. But there is no music.

Enter the conductor. He steps to his podium, lifts his baton, sweeps the scene with his eye, and gives the downbeat. Instantly, there is music. Out of chaos, harmony. Out of bedlam, beauty.

And why? Because the conductor has brought every musician and every instrument into accord with the mind and mood of a great creative artist who may have lived a century or two ago.

How often, in personal life, we are like the orchestra before the conductor enters. Our emotions, attitudes, purposes, loves, and hates are all a jumble within us.

Would that a skilled conductor step to the podium and take control. Would that all the discordant elements be brought into focus upon some noble aim, some high goal. Would that some profound commitment to something worthy of it bring into coordination all our powers and make us whole.

Then perhaps we can make the music we are meant to make. Whom would you have write the score for you? Under whose baton would you have your music made? To whom would you give the instruments of your life? You make your choice, but be aware that many would like the role.

The Rudder That Guides the Ship

If our life may be thought of as a ship, sailing from shore to shore, then what we believe must be considered the rudder that guides it.

The whole voyage, from launching to mooring, requires constant steering, and at every critical point we steer by what we believe in. If we are steering by a star, it's because we believe in the star, in its dependability, its reliability. If we have no fix on a star, we can conveniently convince ourselves of this or that and, in accordance with that conviction, tragically run aground in some dismal and unintended place.

What to believe? It is the oldest of all questions, an issue older than sin. Recall, if you will, that ancient Hebrew story of Adam and Eve and the forbidden fruit. It's the world's second oldest story concerning human behavior. The one older concerns a problem that has proved as enduring as sin and almost as prevalent. The problem is this: What shall I believe?

Remember the story? God told that hapless "First Couple" that if they ate of a certain fruit they would die. Then along came a snake, saying, "Not so; God is deceiving you." Here were two statements, diametrically opposite, both claiming truth. Those two people had a problem, a decision to make. No way could they believe both God and the snake; they had to choose one.

You know the story. They chose the wrong one; they chose to believe the snake, and they acted accordingly. They acted according to what they believed, and they got themselves into terrible trouble for it.

It always works this way. We act according to our beliefs—whether it be a Hitler exterminating the Jews or a Schweitzer treating the sick in Africa. The issue of paramount importance then is this: What shall I believe? And, sometimes, whom shall I believe? If perchance one may choose to say, "I won't believe in anything," this is simply another way of saying, "I believe there's nothing worth believing in." Besides, it must be understood: Should there be such, a rudderless ship will soon run aground or founder in the next upcoming storm.

No question ever asked is more important than this one: What shall I believe? No decision ever made is more critical than the answer to this question. We need to understand that our beliefs are not forced upon us, not ever. We choose them, and the options are more than can be counted.

Choosing what we will believe, knowingly or unwittingly, we are setting the course and establishing the tone of our lives. For example, it was one set of beliefs that made an Adolph Hitler, another that produced an Albert Schweitzer. What we believe can take us to the depths or guide us to the summits. Therefore, on whatever day we browse the smorgasbord of beliefs, let us choose carefully.

A Presence in the Dark

Among the Appalachian hills, at an earlier time, trundle beds were in common use. A trundle bed was a small rollaway bed that in the daytime was pushed under the big bed and at night was pulled out for children to sleep in. As a child I slept in one of those.

Vividly, I remember a troubled night when on my trundle bed there came to me a terrible and frightening dream. In my dream I fought with fiery dragons and fearful pirates and was lost in dark caverns where demons and specters lurked. Awakening terrified, my small body shook with the fear of it all.

Then I felt beneath me an arm, an arm then strong, and I heard a soft, reassuring voice, a voice now silenced for more than sixty years. This was the voice and this the arm of a small boy's mother. There that night, cradled in her arms, I sobbed my way to sleep again. When I next awakened, the breakfast biscuits were baking in the oven and outside the sun was shinning and birds were singing.

That trundle bed, the old log house, the big room that was combined bedroom, kitchen, and living space have now been gone for a long time. But something remains; something remains with me, within me. It abides as an unshakable assurance.

Over the many years that have since passed, in the real world of manhood, with the burdens of life and the pressures of responsibility, other shadows have sometimes closed around me. In the darkness of some dismal place, I have struggled with such dragons as grown men must sometimes wrestle with.

But each time I have felt an arm beneath me, an arm that is never-failingly strong; and I have heard a voice within me, a voice of peace that will not be silenced by any storm. Here I have experienced a truth once told by an ancient sage, this to be found written in the Hebrew book of Deuteronomy, chapter 33, verse 27. This is the word, the reassuring truth: "The eternal God is thy refuge, and underneath are the everlasting arms" (KJV).

DON'T WISH YOUR LIFE AWAY

On Monday, as he begins his week's work, a man says, "I wish it were Friday!" To him, Tuesday, Wednesday, and Thursday are an unimportant interval that he must endure until his coveted Friday arrives. Actually, this man is wishing away three whole days of his life; for when Friday comes, Tuesday and Wednesday and Thursday will have passed, and that wide window of opportunity will have closed forever.

To have time is to have a highly valued possession, and to wish any of it away seems like such a waste. Can Friday be so much better than Monday that one would be willing to give up three whole days of life in order to get to it?

You will never know what next Tuesday can mean until you've had your chance at it and it has had its chance at you. Who knows but that it can turn out to be one of the great days of your life! And, for that matter, so can Wednesday or Thursday. On one of those days a thought may come that will enrich your life forever. On one of those days may come some unheralded messenger of inspiration to lift you a level higher for all your future years. What a difference a day can make!

Three days of life! Who knows what they may bring? In three days Bach can compose an oratorio; in three days Newton can formulate the law of gravitation; in three days Jefferson can write the American Declaration of Independence. And you will not know what *you* can do with three days of life until *you* have lived them through and tried.

If you are willing to wish them away, however, you aren't likely to try very hard, are you? If you see these days as something to have over and be done with, you aren't likely to invest much of yourself in them; neither are you likely to get much dividend from them. You have set the stage for an inconsequentiality!

Our days serve us better when appreciated. We always get along better with a day that we greet warmly and welcome with gusto; we bring more to it and get more from it.

So let's welcome our days and thank them one by one for coming. Some will be better than others, but we'll never know which will be which until sometime later. Let's never, never miss this one while wishing for the next or the next after that.

Yes, it's natural and it's good that we should look forward to future events and times. Hope will often keep us going when other dynamics fail; eager anticipation can brighten a day that can seem otherwise dull and dreary.

But there is always that interval, the distance between the onset of hope and its fulfillment somewhere farther on. The question is: How will we deal with our intervals? Surely we will not wish them away. Intervals also are for living; and if we live them to the full instead of waiting them out, who knows how memorable they may become? The most rewarding life isn't lived from mountain peak to mountain peak, but from day to day.

Neutralizing the Sting

One summer day, while vacationing in Gatlinburg, Tennessee, I went to a neighborhood bait store to purchase some delectable morsels that might prove tempting to the fish in the area. The storekeeper told me about such tidbits as earthworms, crawfish, and minnows. Then she mentioned something that sounded like "wausnes." As it turned out, she was saying "wasp nest." My angling career, limited as it was, had never exposed me to the notion that a piece of a wasps' nest might be so attractive to a fish, but the lady assured me that it is indeed so.

As we talked, the screen door of the little room was abruptly flung open, and in bounded one of the most excited ten-year-olds I have ever seen in motion. Of all things, this little fellow carried in front of him the largest and most perfect wasp nest I have ever seen. As the child rushed up to the counter, the lady stepped back a couple of paces and said somewhat nervously, "Are you sure they're all out of it?" I backed off a couple of paces in the other direction and agreed she was asking a good question. "Yes," the boy replied with a slight suggestion of impatience. "Yes, they're all out, and ain't it a beauty? *And they stung me only once!*"

The storekeeper gave the little fellow a half-dollar, took the nest, and gingerly laid it up on a back shelf. "Thank 'u, ma'am," said the lad, and then with dancing eyes and on dancing feet, he bounded through the doorway and went running down the street.

For no amount of money would I have attempted to take that nest away from its vicious occupants, but that boy had done it! I can hear him yet: "They stung me only once!" Getting stung was merely incidental! Obviously, he had expected to be stung much more than once. But he had been determined to get that nest and that half-dollar, and no amount of stinging was going to make much difference to him.

If we can have that much sheer exuberant enthusiasm about anything, I suppose that getting stung is relatively unimportant. That Gatlinburg lad may be teaching us this: We should always approach any hard task or good cause with enough resolve to neutralize all the stings we may get. If the commitment is deep enough, the wounds are only incidental.

THE IMPLICATIONS OF A WISH

We often wish good things for our friends and those dear to us. We remember them with good wishes, saying, "I hope you have good health…happiness on your birthday…prosperity in the new year."

Doing this, we are, of course, actually wishing beneficial consequences, good results. The good things we wish will not result from our wishing, however. Their realization will depend on other factors. What is it, then, that does produce health, happiness, prosperity? Whatever it is, isn't it this we are really wishing for?

Health? We are saying: "I hope you will behave well, that you will exercise, that you will not abuse your body, that you will eat properly, that you will brush your teeth and keep yourself clean." For it is only by following such patterns of conduct that one can have his or her best chance of enjoying good health.

Happiness? We are saying: "I hope you will think positively, believe in what is good, be affirmative, be thoughtful, be unselfish and helpful to others." For it is only from this kind of living that true happiness usually comes.

Prosperity? We are saying: "I hope you will be diligent, that you will work hard, be honest, use good judgment." For surely prosperity is more likely to result from such industry and diligence than from laziness of any kind or degree.

So, in reality, as we wish such good things as health, happiness, and prosperity for our friends, we are actually giving them a rather important assignment. We are saying: "I hope you will live and think and work in such ways that health, happiness, and prosperity may be yours."

A DISAPPEARING AURA

People who rise above restricting circumstance, who overcome handicaps, who triumph over adversity—we have traditionally admired and applauded them. Horatio Alger struck fire on this flint in 1867 with a story entitled *Ragged Dick*. In his more than thirty years of writing, he produced more than one hundred books, virtually all of them designed for boys and young men. All were tales of courage and high purpose.

Alger's heroes always struggled valiantly against poverty and adversity and always won. It was Alger's idea that by honesty and industry one can rise out of adverse circumstance, succeeding despite the difficulty; the condition of one's birth and early life need not determine one's future.

Enormously popular, these tales of youthful achievement affected nearly two generations of American youth. Many thousands of the underprivileged were inspired to move up from their surroundings or to improve them.

Then came a change. In most academic circles, ideas such as Alger's became rather a laughingstock and were considered naïve and simplistic. Among most of the reform-minded, the concept that one might rise above circumstance was displaced by a concern for the circumstance itself. Mostly, disadvantaged youth were now seen as hopelessly trapped and could not be expected to turn out well. The very idea that by initiative and imagination a young man or young woman might overcome adversity gave way to a kind of social determinism.

Attention was now focused on improving circumstances rather than inspiring youth to improve themselves. Our underprivileged young were now seen as helpless victims caught in a terrible trap. This became a major theme at the cutting edge of social concern. For half a century we have, in effect, persistently told these young that they are hopelessly handicapped. It appears that at length they have come to believe us. Generating in them a sense of futility, we now reap its harvest in the streets and dark alleys of most American cities. Once our young had been inspired to believe in themselves, to rise above and go beyond; now the message they get is mostly gloom and pessimism.

I still believe in our youth. I believe in them because I believe in life. We do youth great harm if we say they haven't a chance. The harm is done the moment the youth hear this said, and they do hear it. Trust them to rise, and most will. Give them reasons to believe in themselves, and watch them abandon street gangs for classrooms and studios and pulpits and corporate boardrooms and ordinary good citizenship.

For the sake of our young, and especially for the sake of our disadvantaged young, I long for the day when the voice of inspiration will be heard again. Youth hungers to hear it and turns away to listen to other voices because the voice of inspiration and encouragement is not much heard anymore.

Of course, we owe it to our young to surround them with the most advantageous circumstances possible. But we also owe it to them to let them know how wonderful and precious their lives are, how packed with possibility, and how exciting the prospects.

MANAGING OUR MINDS

Maybe we don't think of the mind as something to be managed—supposing, perhaps, that it sort of runs on automatic and takes care of itself. It will, of course, if we let it, but it won't serve us well. The mind needs some attention from us.

Five things, I think, might be usefully said about managing our minds.

First: Manage to *use them*. As an unused muscle atrophies, so does the unused mind. As bodies need exercise, so do minds. A mind should be assigned some tasks and expected to perform; and, too, a mind should be trusted to do its job. Use helps keep minds supple, agile, and alert.

Second: Manage to *feed them well*. Like the body, the mind will starve unless fed. Most minds have voracious appetites; they will gobble up almost anything we give them. If they are to be healthy, however, we must be somewhat selective. We must provide them good, wholesome food and a great deal of it. Minds need, especially on occasion, some really meaty stuff. They don't do well on junk foods, but for variety a light, delightful dessert every now and then is a very good thing. But do remember that some things are poisonous and should be avoided totally.

Third: Manage to *keep them open*. The mind that limits itself to the first thing that comes along will miss everything that comes along later. The world is aglow with ever-renewing disclosures. When an insight comes, hold it, but keep a window open for the next one. Truth and revelation make daily treks up and down every street in town, but they enter only at the open doors.

Fourth: Manage to *keep them growing*. Like all living things, minds are made for growth in order to achieve greater capacities and capabilities. Of course, diet has a lot to do with this; properly nourished, minds grow better. They also need exercise; they need challenging tasks and disciplines that sensitize and stretch them.

Fifth: Manage to *control their production*. Yes, the mind is a producer. Like any manufacturing plant, it turns out products. It is in the mind that ideas are spawned, that deep convictions are formed, that vast systems of philosophy are hammered into shape. With possibilities unlimited, the mind can find a way to prevent polio—or it can plan a holocaust. By intricate process, it produces something from the raw materials we send it. Therefore, we need to give most careful attention to the kinds of raw materials with which we stock our minds. Give them something good to work upon, and we can expect good products forthcoming. But if we give them trash, we can't expect much that is worthwhile.

I offer one further notation: Whatever the length of life, minds never outgrow their need for attention. A farmer's crop is said to be "laid by" when, near the end of the growing season, he ceases to cultivate it. Such "laying by" can be a good procedure when dealing with corn or beans, but is not so when dealing with minds. "Laid by," they quickly wither and begin to compose themselves for dying. The longer we can keep the soil stirred, the more productive it will be.

Living by the Light

In deep space, there apparently are areas of such awesome gravitational power that nothing, once attracted to them, can ever escape, not even light. These are called "black holes."

It seems that some minds are like black holes: if anything goes in, it never comes out. Some people will reach out, take something in, and close the door. From then on, whatever comes must go by.

Sometimes we are advised—well advised, actually—to "walk in the light," meaning that we should follow the best guidance we can get. As the years of a lifetime go by, does the amount of available light ever change? Of course it does; more and more, we are flooded by broad, brilliant beams of it. The question is: Will we look with seeing eyes and live by what we see?

Consider the youth (or anyone else) who blunders into a pit, the sloping sides of which are worn smooth by the feet of others who have blundered there before. Someone truthfully says, "You are old enough to know better." Yes, the trail signs had all been in place, warning signs properly posted, the pitfalls well lighted. Yes, he was old enough to know better. By this time, he should have accumulated all the information he needed; it was there and available to him. His fall was not for lack of light. By this time, he should have known.

We keep careful watch over our infant children, don't we? We do so lest they unknowingly fall into dangers we ourselves have long since learned to avoid; we now have more light than do they. Along life's journey, from end to end, the amount of light can vary, usually growing as we go—somewhat as the sun from its rising moves upward to the noon.

You see, whatever the action or the idea, it must be viewed in all the available light at the time. As time goes by, new light comes and comes and keeps coming. This means two things: first, as new light is added, so should we grow; and second, one who would walk in the light must be prepared for change and be willing to accept it.

Whatever may happen along the way, the mind must never become the kind of black hole where whatever gets in will never come out. Over the passing years, some things probably should exit, and other things probably should remain. It is an art of skillful living to know which is which, to know when to hold on and when to let go.

THE HAPPINESS QUOTIENT

In the vocabulary of modern economics, two words have places of paramount importance: *production* and *consumption*; or, in personal terms: *producers* and *consumers*.

Producers are the people who bring things into existence, and consumers are the people who use them up. The words are, of course, most commonly used in reference to *things* such as machines, clothing, food.

Here for a moment, however, let us think about this phenomenon as it operates in another arena of the human experience, namely, the production and consumption of the satisfying qualities of human life. These also are produced and sometimes consumed.

These qualities don't grow like weeds; they must be cultivated—watered, nurtured—produced. Happiness, for instance doesn't just happen. By "happiness" I don't mean pleasure or mere fun, but a genuinely felt sense of well being. It is made up of ingredients intermixed, mingled, combined, and assembled within the human spirit.

I suppose that at any point in time there is in the world only a certain amount of happiness, a certain total. We might think of this as the happiness pool or the happiness quotient. This pool is in constant process of being replenished and diminished, produced and consumed.

Apparently, there are two kinds of people: those who add to the total and those who subtract from it. The level rises and falls as some pour in and others siphon off. Unfortunately, a single dastardly act by one person often destroys happiness in the life of another or even in the lives of many. On the other hand, however, there are those who have ways of making others happy.

Happiness: some people produce it, others consume it—and the happiness the consumers consume is the happiness of other persons. Such consumers are thieves—vandals, actually—and the vandal is the worst of all thieves. There may be horse thieves and automobile thieves and thieves with other specialties, but no thief is more contemptible than the happiness thief, the thief who brutally invades the lives of other people and robs them of this most precious treasure.

On the other hand, how commendable is that pilgrim who in passing adds a touch of happiness here and another there and leaves a trail of happiness behind when gone.

Thankfulness Is a Three-Story House

Most of us have some feelings of thankfulness toward God, or feel that we should. In America, virtually from our beginnings we have annually set apart a day we call "Thanksgiving Day." Although thankfulness is a character trait of most good people, there can be more to it than we often realize.

Visualize thankfulness as a house of three stories, and understand that the truly thankful will occupy the house on all three levels.

We enter on the ground floor. Here we thank God for the miracle, for the remarkable, for the singular event that dramatically turns things around for us. It is the recovery from a terrible illness; it is the rain that comes just in time to save the crop; it is the spectacular deliverance in a time of danger.

This is thankfulness at its most elementary level, a mostly emotional spurt that rises to an occasion and then tends to subside. This occasional kind of thankfulness is the easiest kind; it comes easy, goes easy.

But move up to the second story. Here is thankfulness of the habitual kind. Here thankfulness is a way of life. Here we are thankful for the normal, the ongoing: the continuing good health that made a miraculous recovery unnecessary, the rains that came with such regularity that the crop was never in peril, the fact that we never fell into a danger to be delivered from.

This is thankfulness for the continuing miracle of the natural order, for day-to-day dependability, for the remarkable complex of system and balances in which our life is maintained: the orbiting of planets, the rotation of the earth, sea and land, heat and cold, sunshine and rain, and all the rest.

Going up now to the third story, we encounter a great crystal mirror in which we see ourselves. Here we come to an appreciation of who and what we are. We contemplate the deeps of our own being, the vast area within. We become aware of a remarkable power that is ours, the power to receive into ourselves what comes from without and to convert it into a spiritual quality that we can hold within. Otherwise unknown in the world of living things and unique to our humanity, this is the power that can transpose a fleeting view of a sunset into an inspiration that can last a lifetime. It is the power that can translate the beauty that can be seen or heard into a language the spirit can understand.

Therefore, on this level we give thanks for great music and the ability to hear it and feel it. We give thanks for the rainbow and what the sight of it means within us. Doing so, we are giving thanks for a power that pigs and cattle know nothing about. So, on this level of the three-story house, we give thanks for values that abide within us and for all that helped to put them there, including the people who have blessed us on our way.

May we then think of thankfulness as a three-story house? If so, let us visualize a spacious edifice filled with light and beauty, great winding stairways leading up, broad clear windows looking out, grand entrance doors open wide, this house inviting us to move in and move up and occupy the whole of it.

It's a pleasant place to live, this house, and there are no restrictions as to who may live here. All are welcome, and there is always room for others. Occupants are happy people, affirmative, open, likable. God is pleased to hear from them on a regular basis and is delighted to bless them with more and more good gifts to be thankful for.

Part VIII

Walking Among the Cacti

Somewhere in the mountains of Mexico, we came upon an especially spectacular thicket of cacti. I parked our motor home and got out with camera to explore the possibility of photographs. While others waited, I wandered—not far, but far enough to discover that a cactus can be a formidable foe.

Oh, they were beautiful to look at, those cacti. There were many varieties, intermixed, some in bloom. Cactus blooms can be gorgeous—some small, some large, colors bright with varied hues. Cactus shapes and sizes can vary, ranging from tiny things underfoot to towering monsters.

The most important thing about these cacti, however, is the way they arm themselves for defense, not merely to defend themselves, I think, but also to defend the whole nation of Mexico. These things were equipped either to intimidate an enemy or to take him prisoner.

I didn't know all this when I started out. I knew only that here was a lovely cactus grove and that there should be some nice pictures in it, so I would get them. You know, perhaps, how it is when you are loose with a camera among beautiful things. You want all the angles, various perspectives, the best possible effects.

So I set out to get all this. I didn't get far, however, until I backed into one of those lethal demons. It grabbed my clothing as though it had been waiting since last year for me to arrive, and it held on with spines like fishhooks. While trying to extricate myself from this fiend, I accidentally touched another of another kind, and now had to fight on two fronts.

It was only with the greatest difficulty that I got free, and then I stood discreetly in the clear and looked about—more carefully now. All sorts of diabolical spines, needles, and hooks were everywhere around. I carefully extended a sleeve to within half an inch of one, and I swear the thing bent forward to get me. Of course, I took few pictures there.

Later, I heard local stories of travelers who had been caught by the cacti, were forced to cut away all their clothing, and finally emerged naked and bleeding, near death. Others, not so fortunate as to have knives to cut themselves free, never made it out at all.

Why tell this? Because in some ways, our life, day by day, is a walk among the cacti. If I want to be a person of principle, integrity, and moral quality, I must be wary.

Sometimes, as with that cactus grove, the attractive and the interesting can be most dangerous. Sometimes lethal spines are hidden in colorful and fragrant flowers. Sometimes when we shy away from one peril we can back into another. We can head down narrow paths that dead-end and find it hard to turn around and come back. We can become so engrossed, as I was seeking pictures, that we forget the hazards of the place we travel through.

Yes, if we are to live anywhere in our world, we must walk among the cacti, for they are everywhere. But we can do so if we walk carefully. Exercising prudence and discretion, we can enjoy all that's beautiful and yet avoid the hooks and needles.

AN ETHIC FOR OUR TIME

Right and wrong—many do not speak in these terms anymore. Yet there can be no doubt that some acts are more to be preferred than others. This is confirmed by the fact that we have civil and criminal laws.

Two centuries ago, philosopher Immanuel Kant gave voice to an idea that may be crying out for our attention just now. He wrote: "So act that your principle of action might safely be made a law for the whole world."

In other words, *do* that which, if everybody did, humanity would be the better for it, and *do not do* that which, if everybody did, would be damaging to humanity and at length the utter ruin of us all. It's a rather good guide for personal behavior, is it not? Consider how it would work:

Suppose all people in the world were caring, kind, generous, and wholly given to highest ideals. What a world! But not all people are like this.

Some are liars and covenant breakers. Suppose all were. There could be no commerce, no social institutions, no achievements requiring the efforts of more than one.

Some are sexually promiscuous and unfaithful in marriage. Suppose all were. The very foundation of home and family would be wholly wiped out.

Suppose all were thieves. Where then would be the basis of the mutual trust essential to any sort of social order? How could anyone ever own or manage anything?

Suppose all were murderers. The result would be total anarchy until the last remaining person stood alone in the world.

Some do drugs or drink until life is laid waste. Suppose all did. What then?

It appears, doesn't it, that some people, by their actions, are helping hold the world together; were it not for the integrity of some, there could be no opportunity for any. Others, by their actions, are tearing the world apart, misusing and abusing the arenas of freedom that good people create and maintain.

As seen in relation to any desirable end, some actions are positive, some negative. We are not far amiss, I suspect, to think of the positive as right and the negative as wrong. In any case, Kant's principle of action is this: Never do the thing that, if everybody did it, would be the undoing of us all.

Those among us who have lived very long and have looked upon life with any comprehension at all, will certainly know that the great German philosopher was right. If there are anywhere persons who cannot accept any particular religious ethic or code of morality, one hopes these may at least have sufficient insight to embrace this philosophical one. Having done so, and unknowingly perhaps, they will have embraced the very moral code they had meant to reject.

TESTS FOR BIGNESS IN A MAN

You are a man, and you are *poor*. That is, you have little of money or possession. You labor, your work is hard, and you work extra whenever you can. You count out coins to pay light bills and buy bread. Your child begs for a simple toy that you cannot afford; your little girl cries because she isn't dressed as other girls are. You look at your wife, the woman you love, and you know how her heart would leap and her eyes light up if just once she might have her hair done and be finely dressed. You see it announced that the circus is coming, and you know how your family would love to attend it; but you must stand with them at the curbside, watch the parade go by, and then turn and go home.

Being poor is a problem. It has been the undoing of lesser men. To have almost none of what others have so much is enough to make small men bitter and resentful and vindictive. Being poor is a test of the mettle of which a man is made. You will hurt a lot; you will love a lot; and perhaps you will hurt the more because you love so much.

You are a man, and you are *rich*. That is, you have much of money and possession. There are things that distress you, but by your wealth you are spared the problems that distress the poor man most. You have no anxiety about paying for your family's clothing and food. Your wife and your children can have everything you want them to have. They can go to the circus when it comes, or south in winter, or north in summer, or to Paris or London for the weekend. It is sometimes said of the very poor man that he "is really up against it." But you never are; you are insulated from it. You have the buffer of wealth between you and the realities many men know.

Being rich is a problem. It has been the undoing of lesser men. To have so much of what others have so little is enough to make small men vain and shallow and empty. To find fulfillment in ways that matter, you must somehow get beyond the protective shelter of your wealth, must be in touch with the nitty-gritty. Although your wealth is in some ways a bridge, it is a barrier in others. Some relationships will be clouded by it. Sometimes you will be unsure if your friends are yours or your money's. Some will look on you with suspicion or mistrust, and you will wonder who. Although the poor man is afflicted with one kind of insecurity, you are afflicted with another.

Being rich is a test of bigness in a man, and only big men pass it. To do so, you will see to it that outward quantity does not usurp the place of quality within; you will forbid your wealth to buffer you too much against the pains of your fellow men; and you will maintain always a clear distinction between all the artificial that you can buy and all the real that you cannot.

Both poverty and riches are tests for bigness in a man. In either case, a man must be bigger than his circumstance. The truly big man, if poor, would be equally as big if rich, and the truly big man, if rich, would be equally as big if poor. The dimensions of a man are not measured by what is around him, but by what he is within.

New Versions of an Ancient Art

You and I have seen many changes in our lifetime, some for the better, some not so, and as for some we don't know yet. Look with me now at one of these changes. I ask you, in which category does it fall? Let's think about a sense of personal responsibility, the way ideas have changed about it and are yet changing.

Time was when each of us was deemed fully responsible for his or her own actions. Lately, however, we have revived some long-dormant tactics to excuse ourselves from such responsibility.

The ancient Hebrew idea of the scapegoat we now regard as primitive superstition. Nevertheless, in our time we are wont to lay our guilt or blame on a whole herd of such goats—and we keep the herd conveniently at hand. We rely heavily on these to relieve ourselves of responsibility for our bad behaviors, and society is as prone to do this for us as we are to do it for ourselves.

Consider the man who has developed an utterly despicable pattern of antisocial conduct. Why does he behave this way? Once it would have been said that such a fellow was a bad man, but not now, not usually anyway. We now look for other places to put the blame.

For instance, we may blame his genes. We may say he inherited his faults from his ancestors and is therefore to be excused. The fault is not in his will but in his genes, it is sometimes said; the issue isn't moral, it's biological. We have here a kind of biological determinism. Poor fellow, his genes made him do it. But one must wonder: Did the man do everything possible to overcome his genetic debility? Hadn't he an obligation to do so?

Another twist in this escape phenomenon puts the blame on society, on other people, all of us. Ignoring the fact that other neighborhood children turned out splendidly, there are those who will say this fellow never had a chance. He must therefore be thought of as a victim, and the failure is ours, not his.

Or perhaps the blame is laid on the poverty goat, the rationale being that the man behaved so badly because he had to grow up poor. Well, for that matter, so did Abraham Lincoln, George Washington Carver, and several million other fine and successful folks. Isn't it possible that what we bring to our circumstances may have something to do with the way we allow them to affect us?

We might go on to name a good number of other goats to which we often assign our guilt or blame, rather than assume it ourselves. Instead, let us note an important historical fact:

A few thousand years ago, as a study of all ancient cultures will reveal, people sought to avoid responsibility by attributing their actions to forces beyond themselves. They did what they did because the gods or demigods were in control. The gods made them do it; they were pawns in hands other than their own. We don't believe in these gods or demigods anymore; we consider ourselves too sophisticated for that. But haven't we come up with some pretty good substitutes?

The Walls We Build

Not with hammer and trowel, but by repeated acts of will, we are forever building walls. Not with bricks and mortar, but with the materials of day-to-day experience, we surround ourselves with barricades, walling some things in and others out.

All through our years the process goes on, as the walls we build are dismantled here and reconstructed there, as they are pushed out or pulled in on the various perimeters of our lives. Whether the traffic would go out or come in, we position our sentries atop the ramparts, there to shout the age-old challenge: "Thou shalt not pass!" By these walls of ours, we include or exclude certain ideas, loyalties, interests, attitudes, and sometimes other persons.

Of course, even as the gardener may need a fence about his garden to keep the varmints out, I need some protective walls around my life. Lurking out there in the shadows are packs of ugly, brutal, monstrous things that, should they get in, would lay me waste. There are notions and practices running loose in the world that I must be on guard against. My integrity and my virtue are treasures worth defending, and so I do need a line of defense against the vandals and thieves who would desecrate or steal. To shelter the sacred precincts of my life, I need some walls about me.

But prisons, too, are made of walls, and walls can block the flow of air and flood of light. If they are made of the wrong materials and put in the wrong places, I can suffocate behind the walls I build. If I build of fear, I likely make a prison for myself; this is not so if I build of faith. Walls made of prudence will have one effect, and those made of prejudice will have another. Prejudice and fear make dreadful prisons for those who wall themselves so tightly in.

The secret, then of successful walling is to build so closely in as to protect all that is precious and so far out as to encompass all that is good.

Never Get Off the Train in a Tunnel

The great passenger train skirts the mountainsides, thunders around the curves, through the cuts, across the bridges, and then, approaching the side of a mountain, turns abruptly into it. It's a tunnel. Inside all is dark, all sounds are louder, and there is, among the passengers, a feeling of being closed in. The timid cease their conversations.

In a matter of moments, somewhere deep inside the mountain, the darkness slowly turns to gray, then there is a sudden burst of light, and the powerful machine breaks out into the world beyond.

In our journey of life, also, there are tunnels. How often it happens that life's express is racing onward—along the level plains, up the steep climbs, across the rugged heights, sweeping alongside the mountains—and then, abruptly, turns into the dark. Troubles are upon us, trials press in, sorrows tear at the heart, suffering obscures our sun, and songs of joy give way to pain. Our life has come to a tunnel.

Every tunnel, however, has two ends; there is the end to go in at and the end to come out by. Having gone in, we will come out—unless. We will come out unless we get off in the tunnel. Who, however, would do that? It's dark in there, and damp, and cold, and a miserable place to be.

Nevertheless, and sadly, some who come to tunnels do get off the train in them. In a time of trial, a moment of depression, they get off the train in there in the dark and let it go on without them. There, in bitterness or self-pity, they sit and pout as the years go flying by and time is running out. In a very real sense, they give up on living.

Whoever will go anywhere must necessarily have some impetus for the going—a faith, a confidence that out there is something worth going for. When we are traveling by faith and come to a tunnel of trouble, this is not the time to abandon the faith we have traveled by.

Wherever we are going, we need a faith that will take us there. There will probably be some tunnels on the way, and our faith must be strong enough to take us thorough them. Traveling by such a faith, we will know certainly, when comes a tunnel time, that if we only stay on board and wait, we will come out at length into the sunlight beyond the mountain.

Tall Enough to Touch the Stars

I will never forget the day Professor William L. Stidger walked into our Boston University classroom, placed his books on his desk, looked at us students, and said, "God believes in me, and this faith in me has lifted me up until I have been tall enough to touch the stars."

God believes in *me*! Here was a thought that had never until then entered my mind, but on this day it struck like a thunderbolt. I had thought much about my believing in God, but not at all about God's believing in me. I have thought a great deal about it since, and I see evidences of its truth everywhere abounding.

For instance, I am entrusted with the strength to lift an arm. God knows that, having this power, I can reach out and bless my fellow man, or I can made a fist of my hand and beat him into the dust. Letting me have such power, God is taking a terrific chance on me. Surely he must believe in me that I will use this power well.

I have the power of choice. I am entrusted with it, and I am given more than half a century of years in which to use it. Strength and time—these are allowed me, and both are dangerous to possess.

I am trusted, and I am moved and empowered by that trust. If being trusted cannot stir the heroic in me, then what can? Being believed in ought to move me to commitment and faithfulness. If I have even a smidgen of the character that belongs to human personhood and if someone believes in me, I will strive with all my might never to betray that trust. I will be inspired and fired and lifted by that belief, whoever it is who believes—my parent, my spouse, my child, my friend, anyone, and especially God.

So I believe I know what the professor meant that day on Boston's Beacon Hill: "God believes in me, and this faith in me has lifted me up until I have been tall enough to touch the stars."

In Defense of Dreaming

When I speak of dreaming I do not mean the kind we do while we sleep, but the kind we do when we are most awake and a magnificent upward urge takes hold and tugs at the soul.

Yes, I know that ours is an age that doesn't take well to dreaming. It's a practical and pragmatic age, and I fear that "the stuff that dreams are made of" is not one of the most highly advertised commodities of our time. But whatever the age or time, there ought to be a place from dreaming in it, and I will staunchly defend its right to be there.

Dreaming, you see, is a function of our highest nature, our better selves, and I suspect that not one of us is ever really a full person unless at some time he or she is possessed by a dream. It is as though there is within us a singular compartment made for dreams to live in, and we are never wholly alive unless, at lease once, a dream has lived there.

Our dreams can become ladders by which we climb. Dreams, it seems, have eyes and by these we see what otherwise we miss. Dreaming, then, can be the breakaway window of escape from the narrow stockades of our persistent littleness.

Perhaps the dream window is the only one through which the highest summits may ever be seen, and we do need to see them. Mostly, we live in narrow valleys; we need to look up, and one who dreams does.

Of course, unfulfilled, our dreams can go by in default. They often do, but the soul is a little cleaner because a dream has passed through.

Have you ever considered that only within the human spirit is a dream ever nurtured into life, and only here can that life be sustained? No qualifications are specified. Anyone can dream; and often the loftiest dreams are nurtured in the spirits of those in most lowly places. Often, too, those dreams have become ladders for climbing.

When it comes to dreaming, anyone can be original, anyone can create. It may well be that the only thing uniquely yours, the only thing you will ever actually create or produce, will be the dream that comes to life within you and lives within your heart.

WHEN COMES A COLD TATER TIME

Visiting in the Appalachian hills, I attended a community gathering. During the proceedings, a mountain boy sang a number I had never heard and have never forgotten: "Take a Cold Tater and Wait."

I was reminded of my own childhood at our family farm home. When company came, sometimes numbering a dozen or more at a time, there was a special problem with meals and a kind of protocol. The older and more important guests were called to eat at the "first table." When these had finished, others were called to take their turn, and so it was until all were fed, the children always being the last served. Hence we have the song "Take a Cold Tater and Wait" ("Tater," of course, means "potato").

Think of it now: In the ongoing process of our living, do we not every once in a while come to our cold tater times: times when things aren't going well, times when it seems everything has come to a standstill, when all forward movement has been arrested?

The question: What shall we do when comes such a time? For one thing, we might simply and gracefully accept this as one of life's givens; we just cannot have everything we want the way we want it and when.

Another thing we might profitably do is take our cold tater and walk out by the yard fence and watch the roses bloom, or go down by the brook and see the minnows swim, or sit on the front porch and hear the brown thrush sing from his perch among the maple leaves. Doing so, it may turn out after all that a cold tater along with roses, minnows, and a brown thrush can be better and more rewarding than fried chicken could ever have been.

Dealing with the Usual

The service station attendant was a lithe, alert, open-faced young man whom I had not previously met. When I drove my car into his station and asked him to make repairs on a tire, he agreed with a smile to do so and set to it with a will.

Almost immediately, however, the signal bell sounded, and the young man rushed away to pump gas for a customer. He soon came again to work on my tire; but again the bell rang, and another customer was waiting at the pump. While I waited, the young attendant, working the station alone, must have been called from the tire to the pumps at least a dozen times. Under difficult circumstances, he did the best he could.

The repair work, at last, was finished. As I paid him and as he wiped the sweat from his face with his sleeve, he said apologetically, "I'm sorry it took longer than usual, but then it usually does." My newly met friend seemed not to realize what he had said until an instant after he said it. Then, as it dawned, he grinned a bit sheepishly, shrugged, and turned to his next customer.

It usually takes longer than usual! How about that? It is usually more difficult than usual. So what? It made no difference to this young man; he will go right on repairing tires and, when necessary, pumping gas.

Next time, as last time, he will go right on assuming cheerfully the assigned task, and he will reckon with circumstances as they come up. If it usually takes longer than usual, well, what of it? He'll tackle the job anyway, and he'll get it done. He'll do it with a smile—and everybody around him will also smile—and the world will be a little brighter and a little better.

A Light for Seeing

Nothing is really seen until viewed in a proper light. Looking at any person, situation, question, or issue, it is essential to ask: In what light am I seeing?

Look at a brook-bottom stone through clear-flowing water, and you will not see the object as it is, but a distortion that light has made because of having passed through the ripples. Unfortunately, many elements that can infest our human minds and spirits are equally light-refracting. Look at any person through the prism of prejudice or bitter experience, and you are likely not to see the person at all, but a distortion of what that person really is.

Mostly, we see through lenses, and so often these are light-refracting and therefore distorting. We look, and we glibly say, "So this is what it looks like." Actually, however, we cannot say that we have truly seen anything or anyone until we have asked and honestly answered this question: Was the light right?

In 1922 Daniel French's magnificent statue of Lincoln was unveiled in Washington, D.C. But there was a problem. Because of improper lighting, the face was garishly distorted. Not until the lighting was made right could the statue be seen as it really was. Looking at persons or issues, if we are to see clearly, it is sometimes necessary that we correct our faulty lighting.

WAILERS AND WALKERS

A good story comes to us from about thirty-five hundred years ago. Moses had brought the Israelites out of Egypt and to the edge of the Red Sea. Their slavery past, those people were now on their way to their "promised land." But theirs was now a precarious situation. Before them loomed the sea, and behind them the hostile armies of Egypt were closing in. Within them seethed an awful restlessness, a resistance, a hopelessness, a despair.

In this desperate hour Moses prayed. God said to him: "Why are you crying to *me*? Speak to the *people* that they go forward!" Well, Moses did speak, and the people did go. Somehow the water divided and let them pass.

Now here was an occasion when God told a man to stop praying and start acting, to get off his knees and onto his feet. Moses was looking toward God, but God turned him around. God said to him: "You speak to the people, and you tell them it's time to stop wailing and start marching."

There is no record that Moses argued. He didn't say, "But, Lord, look at all that water!" He got up and spoke, and the people got up and went, and in some way the water let them go through.

The story has a sequel. About forty years later, Joshua stood with those same people on the east bank of the Jordan River. That river was at flood stage, and the "promised land" lay just beyond.

Joshua commanded the people to line up for the crossing. Many assumed, I suppose, that they would be swept into the Dead Sea. But Joshua did a strange thing. Usually the soldiers led the march, but this time he put the priests at the head of the column. When the feet of those men touched the water, in some way the river opened and let the people cross to the other side.

I don't understand how this happened, but I do have a feeling about it: If those priests had not walked into the water as though it would open, it wouldn't have opened.

There is, however, something about all this that I believe I do understand. In the journey of our living, we often come to our Red Seas and our Jordan Rivers, and the crossing seems difficult or impossible. But I do know this: No sea or river is ever going to let you cross it until you *attempt* the crossing. Whatever the limiting, restricting circumstance, the time comes for us to break camp and start marching, when we must stop wailing and start walking.

How Long or Short Is Time?

Time, so it seems, is both long and short—long by the day and short by the life span.

On the day-by-day basis, time goes somewhat indifferently by. At 9:30 it can seem like a long while until the break for lunch and even longer until dinner. When will the workday end, and will Friday never, never come? The start of that scheduled vacation—it seems so far away. Whatever we want of tomorrow, it always seems a long time coming.

This is especially so when we are very, very young and looking forward to a lot: Christmas, the next birthday, when school is out. When we are eleven, how we long to be twelve, and when twelve or fourteen, we long for sixteen. Always, of course, what we long for seems a long time coming, and so time moves for us at the pace of a lazy snail out for an afternoon stroll.

As we grow older, however, responsibilities multiply. There are duties to do, schedules to keep, deadlines to be met, and it seems that all such come rushing upon us at attack speed. So the pace of time accelerates; its spaces, such as minutes, hours, and days, seem now to have grown shorter than they used to be.

However, when many years, at whatever speed, have passed, we look back upon them and can scarcely believe what we see. All those years—where have they gone—and so quickly?

One Marvelous Summer Morning

It was an early summer morning, about midway between midnight and dawn, and I was alone, driving eastward along a Midwestern country road. Alongside, all the farm homes were yet dark; and above, the stars were bright. In the north, though, a cloud was rising. As I drove I observed it rise and saw it grow larger and larger until it filled the whole northern third of sky.

I heard no thunder but saw lightning flashes—not the sharp boltlike kind that come crashing down to earth, but the sheetlike kind that play among the clouds. Fascinated, I drove more and more slowly as I watched, until at last I pulled off the road, turned off the headlights, got out of the car, and stood silently at the roadside, transfixed by all I was seeing.

It must have been half an hour or more that I stood there viewing a spectacle of light and color unlike anything I had ever seen. The entire northern sky was alive with it. Ever-changing, never predictable, and wholly without sound, fantastic cloudscapes were illuminated in momentary flashes—here a great, craggy mountain in silhouette, there intricate patterns of lace, and yonder vast, meandering caverns—shape superimposed upon shape, color upon color, accented and backlighted, layered and tiered—overpowering in dimension and depth, all majestically beautiful, as may be vistas from another world.

There was I, alone, confident that I was the only human creature in this entire world seeing precisely what I saw or who would ever in all of time see what I saw.

Strange feelings mingled within me. As I tried to understand them, one realization came more clearly than all others: I see all this beauty, and yet I feel so sad. Why?

More than anything else, it was indeed a deep sadness that I felt. At first I wondered about it and worried a little. Then slowly, understanding came: *I see all this beauty, but there is no one with whom to share it.*

Thirty-nine years have passed since then, and I have often reviewed and reconsidered the melancholy I felt in that hour. Why should the absence of another person have been so important to me? I'm sure I don't know. Psychologists may take the question and make something of it. But as for me, I know only that I was terribly lonely, that I deeply missed some-body. I don't know why.

But this I do know: In the magnificent light of that marvelous summer morning, I saw something I had largely overlook before—the enormous meaning of other people in my life.

Usually I have someone with whom to share a beauty or a joy. Until that morning, however, I think I had not really understood the meaning of this, what a wonderful difference it makes. Normally, there are those some-where near to stand with me when I am weak or to weep with me when I cry, but it was only after I had felt the sadness of that strange predawn that I got some inkling of what my life would be like without them.

The truth is this: Over these many years, many fellow human beings have walked beside me, have stood with me, have entered into my life and let me enter theirs. They have been with me in springtime sun and when dark storms have raged around me and within. They have freely and feelingly given me a hand when I have reached for one. They have been there to share with me the wonder and majesty of our common life. If I could speak with each today, I would say thank you and bless you for all you've meant to me.

The Winds and the Waiting

A friendly wind feels its way across the harbor, a wind seeking a sail. But the ships are all at anchor, the sails all furled. In vain the wind goes by.

A ship rides the open ocean swells, its sails all spread to catch a wind. But the wind does not come, no air is stirring; and the ship lies waiting.

This is life—the seeking, searching everywhere; the reaching, yearning, striving, trying—a wind seeking a sail, and a sail seeking a wind.

However, then comes the momentous day when wind and sail are brought together. The limp canvas billows full, all hands rush to places, and the ship's sharp prow slices its way through the rolling, living sea.

This, too, is life, for life is some of both, both the wind and the waiting. Two things, therefore, one who would live must learn: how to wait and how to set sail.

The Plainville Formula

About thirty years ago, driving along a country road in southern Wisconsin, we came upon a small airplane parked in a farm field just beyond the roadside fence. There was the suggestion of a landing-strip out across the field. Nearby, a homemade windsock fluttered from a ten-foot pole, and there was a small backyard type of shed that could probably house a barrel of gasoline and few other small items. Nothing else was in view—nothing, that is, except a small, bold sign affixed to the fence. As we read that sign, we enjoyed a good laugh. It read: "Plainville International Airport."

As our laughter subsided, however, I realized that I felt a strong tide of joy arising within me. I felt warm and pleased and thrilled somehow. Why? At first I scarcely knew, but then I found myself wishing I could meet the fellow who owned that airplane. He must be a fascinating sort, I thought. Certainly, he must have a delightful sense of humor. But there was more: optimism, obviously, and a kind of buoyant scorn of circumstances.

I didn't meet the fellow, but I like him, and I've had thirty years to think about him. I like the spirit of the man. Plainville International Airport! It suggests to me a lighthearted redemption of the commonplace, a kind of sublimation of what is routine, a priceless ornamentation of the ordinary— the internationalization of anyone's Plainville!

Yes, our day-to-day can be quite plain, commonplace, ordinary. But if we live it by the Plainville Formula, it won't be boring anymore.

Shall I ever again despise the day of small things? I think not. However small those things may be, I think I will just give them wings and fly them— out of an "international airport" of my own—right here in my own "Plainville." I, too, would like to hang a sign on the fence and look out upon the world and smile.

THE WHITTLING

The beautiful mountain country where I grew up represented life at its bare bones. There was no electricity, no natural gas, no telephones, no televisions, no daily newspapers, no paved roads, no school buses, no central heat or running water in houses, and the occasional automobile was a curiosity. Life was no-frills, basic, right down to the essentials.

Among my memories, a very small thing looms large—the whittling. The pocket knife was a sort of symbol of masculinity; every man and boy had one. In that rural area, knives were useful at times. But their most common use served no practical purpose at all—just whittling.

Virtually every knife owner was a whittler; that is, he whittled with no interest in making anything. He whittled just for the sake of whittling. I'm not sure why he whittled, and I'm not sure he knew, and I don't think he needed to know. He whittled while he talked, he whittled while he thought; while he *lived* he whittled. It was an essential sort of living, basic, no-frills.

When two men met on a road or a path or in a field, at least one soon had knife in hand, whittling on a stick or a fence rail or whatever was handy, and not long after the other would be doing the same. While the two talked business or visited about the weather or shared the community news, they whittled. To me, it always seemed impossible to whittle and not be thoughtful. I observed, too, that no one ever whittled in a hurry.

The porch of Arnott's general store was the whittler's Mecca. On the porch was a bench and several cane-bottom chairs, and along the outer edge, from post to post, ran a rail made of wood. That rail, as men whittled at it, changed shape year by year until finally it was almost whittled away.

Along with their knives, men often carried small pieces of wood in their pockets. Often when two or three or more congregated on the porch or anywhere, out came both knife and wood, and the whittling began. The whittling was rarely, if ever, a topic of conversation. The men talked of other things or of nothing at all. As for the whittling, it called for no comment.

Well, whittling must surely have been an effective relaxant. When whittling, it's hard to be uptight about anything or mad at anybody. You see, ours was whittling country; and in all the years I was a part of it, I never heard of anyone having a nervous breakdown. Between whittling and working, somewhere we found a balance, and somehow we held together.

It's now been years since I saw anyone whittling, and I think I miss seeing that. We live now in a different age, and I suspect that maybe we need to whittle more.

When Life Puts You on Hold

Mr. Smith is a busy businessman in a busy business office, but you feel it urgent that you speak with him. You pick up your phone and dial the number. "I'll connect you," says a voice from the other end. Shortly, another voice says, "Mr. Smith's office; may I help you?" You say, "I wish to speak with Mr. Smith, please." Immediately, the voice demands, "Who's calling?" You give the voice your name. After the briefest of pauses, the voice says, "Mr. Smith is on another line; wait a moment please; I'll put you on hold."

Then at the other end of that long wire, a switch is flipped or a button is pushed, and you wait, and you wait, and you wait. The line is dead, temporarily dead, you hope. You wait; and there is no clue as to what is happening at the other end. Are you disconnected? Will someone speak again? If so, when? You wait, afraid to hang up, for any second now somebody will surely say something from over there. You fidget and you fret, but mostly you wait. You wait for a connection, for a voice, for something to start happening. You wonder if you are being ignored, overlooked, or forgotten, or if somehow your call has gone amiss. When, if ever, will things begin to go forward for you?

Well, in the ongoing course of our lives, it seems that sometimes somebody pushes a hold button. It's an illness, an accident, a calamity, an interruption of some sort, and we are put on hold. Everything comes to a standstill, and there we are. We want things to go on, we want things to move, but we see nothing happening; we want to go ahead, but something about life is saying, "Wait." We want our anxieties answered, but life is saying, "Not yet." We want our hopes realized, our dreams fulfilled, and somehow they are not.

The question is: What shall we do when life puts us on hold? The answer, I think, is this: Hold on! Whatever happens or doesn't happen, when you come to a holding time, don't hang up; hang on. Hang on and wait, and keep on waiting, and don't give up. Keep yourself prepared, expectant, hopeful; for sooner or later, the lines will open again, and a voice will say, "We're ready now," and life will go on. I do mean "on" and on and on, if only you hold on.

Hold onto what? you may ask. This depends, of course, on what you have to hold onto—what confidence, what assurance, what faith, what certainty. The stronger that is, the more secure you will be. Actually, the faith that is great enough for any circumstance is the faith that in good times you have held so firmly that in bad times it will hold you.

LOVE'S ROAD IN RETROSPECT

When I look back over the road we've come,
  Scan all the grandeur that looms in view,
I thrill again to the beauty of all I see—
  Those precious miles I've walked with you.

There stand the summits we scaled together,
  There the peaceful paths we wandered hand in hand;
It was the spring, our starlight and roses time,
  And there, charmed, we dreamed and planned.

There lie the dim, dark valleys that we passed;
  I see them clearly now, more clearly now than then.
Somehow, together we came through, didn't we,
  And broke with joy out into the light again.

This, our journey, has been my life, my song.
  It's evening now, and in evening's mellow glow,
The road lies yet clear beneath the twilight sun,
  Miles of memories, rainbows from long ago.

So, today as I look back, this I know:

No love more precious could I have found,
  Though I'd searched the whole creation through,
Nor could there have been for me a better way
  Than to have walked this road with you.

Alphabetical Index